If there's a book that you want to read,

but it hasn't been written yet, then you must write it.

~ Toni Morrison

You have to write the book that wants to be written.

And if the book will be too difficult for grown-ups, then you write it for children.

~ Madeleine L'Engle

A word after a word after a word is power.

~ Margaret Atwood

HEINLEIN'S BUSINESS RULES

1. You must write.

2. You must finish what you write.

3. You must refrain from rewriting except to editorial order.

4. You must put it on the market.

5. You must keep it on the market until sold. (In the new publishing environment, keeping it on the market means to refresh the covers and front/back matter every six years or so.)

Omnium rerum principia parva sunt.

The beginnings of all things are small.

Discovering Your Novel

Think like a Pro Writer series :: 4

by M. A. Lee

Writers Ink Books

Discovering Your Novel

Think like a Pro Writer series

Copyright © 2019 Emily R. Dunn doing business as M.A. Lee & Writers' Ink

First electronic publishing rights: March 2019

NOTE FROM THE AUTHOR

This book is a work of non-fiction. Any names, characters, places, and incidents of fiction and nonfiction are cited by the author merely as explanation. Any persons or entity, existing or dead, are also cited by the author for the purposes of explanation. The author does not have any control over and does not assume any responsibility for third-party websites or their content.

Published in the United States of America

Cover design by Deranged Doctor Design

www.writersinkbooks.com

winkbooks@aol.com

OTHER BOOKS BY M.A. LEE

NON-FICTION

Think like a Pro Writer series

Think like a Pro: New Advent for Writers (1)

Think/Pro: A Planner for Writers (2)

Old Geeky Greeks: Write Stories with Ancient Techniques (3)

*2 * 0 * 4 Lifestyle: A Planner for Living*

FICTION

Into Death series

Digging into Death

Christmas with Death

The **Hearts in Hazard** series

A Game of Secrets (I)

A Game of Spies (II)

A Game of Hearts (III)

The Dangers of Secrets (IV)

The Dangers for Spies (V)

The Dangers to Hearts (VI)

The Key to Secrets (VII)

The Key for Spies (VIII)

The Key with Hearts (IX)

The Hazard of Secrets (X)

The Hazard for Spies (XI)

The Hazard with Hearts (XII)

M.A. Lee's Amazon page can be found at https://www.amazon.com/M.A.-Lee/e/B019PD3Z7W/

CONTENTS

THE DISCIPLINE OF WORK

Designed to develop a novel in one year, this writers' craft book will easily adjust to your own pace. Speed up, slam on the brakes, detour, or meander onto side roads, your drive to a completed novel is under your total control.

The guidelines presented in *Discovering Your Novel* will set an achievable pace of one hour each day, five days every week, whether the hour is a single block of time or in 15-minute stretches.

Cruise through what you know or inch along in your traffic of words, *Discovering Your Novel* will help you achieve indie publication—or set you on the seemingly different path to traditional publication which still uses the same crafting and marketing techniques.

Discovering Your Novel will guide writers of any variety, from pantsters to plotters to puzzlers and mosaic tilers, wherever the Muse leads.

PERSISTENCE

Write 5 days in every week, in 1-hour or 1 ½-hour increments. Plan to take two days off as "rest".

On those two days when no writing occurs, let the ideas swirl around. Brainwork followed by rest allows creativity to flourish.

We all want long blocks of time; those rarely occur. One hour, every evening (or morning) is do-able.

Record your daily word counts and track your progress. When we're tired, we often feel like we're not accomplishing anything. The word counts and progress tracking confirms that we are succeeding.

Life does happen. When it does, re-consider those two rest days. The **it days when you couldn't write on your current project? Those become your rest or creativity days. Flip them out to maintain persistent increments.

Or avoid the five days of the week and do everything on the weekend—although life should happen. Don't turn into a writing hermit. Relationships and events feed creativity.

Two mindsets belong to the professional writer. 1] Make the writing schedule fit your life. 2] Meet your writing deadlines.

Persist at this incremental level, and the pages turn into scenes which become chapters that build into a book.

Look what persistence does. In one session, can you write 1,000 words? (That's two 500-word essays. You can do essays, right?)

- A page of double-spaced writing is about 285 words.
- Four pages of this is about 1,000 words.
- 1,000 words in five days is easy math = 5,000 or a chapter, basically.
- Five days a week over one month is at least 20 days (or four weeks) = 5,000 x 4 = 20,000 words or 70 pages.
- In 3 ½ months you can write about 75,000 words.
- A 265-page manuscript of 285 words per page = 75,525 words. That's a novel.

The word-count and page-count rack up quickly. HOWEVER, these counts depend on three things:

1) That you understand the novel writing process (Foundation).
2) That you know the story that you will write (Visioning).
3) That you listen to your own head and heart (Analysis).

FINISH

The majority of people who launch a book never finish it. NEVER. They may have dozens of stories started—and none finished.

Finishing is BIG. The conclusion of a novel is a completely different skill than the opening of one. If you never finish, you never practice that concluding skill in order to improve it.

The sense of satisfaction that comes from finishing such a large project drives you to complete the next part of writing: revision. After which comes enhancement. Then proofreading. And final corrections.

You need to know the complete track of the story before you look for the gaping errors with plot and character switcheroos. You need to ensure that foreshadowing works. You need to check for pacing.

For enhancement, you might want a little word play—the important word here is "little". Don't knock the reader out of your story with distracting words and phrases. You might want to weave in a motif related to a character: like the snaky villain or the angelic mentor. *Venom* and *fangs* and *slithery* as well as *halo* and *winged messenger* and *bright with knowledge* are simple touches that won't disrupt the flow of reading. For mysteries, you need to ensure you have red herrings and distractors from the true murderer.

Proofreading is essential. No one is 100% perfect, and errors will occur. You can limit errors by reading backwards, a page at a time. Objective distance from the story is also essential to spotting errors in your final corrections.

CRITIQUE GROUPS

Some people live and breathe by their critique groups. Pro writers do not. While they may have a few people that they call in when they're stumped, they have developed a major skill: the ability to trust their own writing. Newbie writers may need critique groups to give them objective feedback. Pro writers have developed their analytical skills.

Pro writers call on the necessary people when they've finished a manuscript. They want people who will spot plot holes and character discrepancies, judge pacing and diss the flowery language that shouldn't be typed onto the page.

Yes, I know all the arguments for critique groups. They can be a wonderful reinforcement for newbie writers who are hesitant. A dependable group can be wonderful for brainstorming and solving problems. A supportive group will listen when you vent.

Unless you are blessed with a critique group that is filled with professional writers in your particular genre, however, you are listening to the wrong people. You need to listen to *published* writers.

Ideally, a group will read the whole manuscript before critiquing. Please don't take a single chapter once a month to a critique group and ask for guidance. A chapter at a time is far from great; it's actually detrimental. People forget. People lose track. A midlister comes in for one meeting, gives great advice that doesn't take into account anything that's gone before, then doesn't return for the next month.

Writers who depend on their critique groups also wind up writing by committee. They listen and revise then revise again and again. Then they repeat that process. They get hung up on one sentence rather than the whole picture.

Worst of all, critique groups can become a crutch. You never learn for yourself. You focus on their ideas rather than your own writing, your own story, your own plans.

Writer organizations are essential. Groups abound that defend writers and their interests, that band together at conferences, host seminars, and dispense wisdom. Yet Romance Writers of America and Sisters in Crime and similar organizations do not have a place in your daily writing.

DISCIPLINE

Planner / Plotter / Pantster / Puzzler / Muse Muffin—whether you use the mosaic method or a chronological one, whether you outline every scene or let the words flow, the method does not matter. Discipline matters.

Find the writing situation that works for you. Leaned back in a recliner typing away, typing in a quiet corner or a busy coffeehouse, handwriting your ideas into a rough shape, dictating the first draft then adding in and fixing machine errors: whatever works.

Plug away at the daily word count. On some days the words will have wings; on others, you're mining through bedrock. Never write until you are drained; stop with energy and ideas still to come.

As for those ideas that still are coming: jot them down at the end of your writing session. For writers, this is a time-honored discipline. Your subconscious will begin working on those ideas. When you start the next session, the words are there. Create a hot list for the session and go.

Writer's Block doesn't exist. If you think you have it, just write the next sentence and the next and the next. Before you know it, you've rolled through a half-page. The blank page is no longer a spiraling vulture eating your writing time.

We are never truly blocked. I devoted a chapter to the fallacy of Writer's Block in *Think like a Pro*, book one of this series. We can always write, whether it's an email or a text or an analysis for work. We just may not want to write what we should.

The best discipline for writers is to memorize Heinlein's Rules. These are five simple yet powerful decrees that should govern your writing life. Robert Heinlein called these business rules; they keep writers productive. They will seem easy. They aren't.

FOUNDATIONS

Record word and page counts, even when developing ideas rather than actually writing manuscript pages. These counts provide a sense of accomplishment.

Never delete the ideas that you develop. On Wednesday, you may decide to trash your writing; by Friday you may want those ideas back. Even if the ideas stay trashed, they may seed another book. Store any deleted work in an *ideas folder*.

WEEK	FOCUS	START DATE	END DATE	HOURS SPENT	WORD COUNT	PAGE COUNT
1	PICK					
2	SKETCH					
3	KNOW A					
4	KNOW B					
5	BUILD					

Total Number of Days Spent Writing :: ....
Total Word Count for Foundations :: ....
Average Number of Words per Day :: ....
Total Page Count for Foundations :: ....
Average Number of Pages per Day :: ....
Actual Page Count for Novel (not research) :: ....
Actual Word Count for Novel (not research) :: ....

As the story develops, these beginning ideas may change and even transform. Story is organic and fluid; let it grow and flow.

FOR THOSE WORKING WITH THE E-BOOK VERSION, CREATE YOUR OWN TEMPLATE OF THE MAJOR CHARTS

OR DOWNLOAD THEM FROM WWW.WRITERSINKSERVI.COM WEBSITE, UNDER THE PRO WRITER ADVICE PAGE.

WEEK 1 :: PICK YOUR NOVEL

COMPLETION CHART

DAY / DATE	FOCUS ~ BRIEF INFO	PAGE COUNT	WORD COUNT	SESSION TIME
1	IDEA			
2	STORY			
3	PROTAGONIST			
4	ANTAGONIST			
5	THEME			
6	CATCH-UP DAY			
7	REST / PLANNING			
	TOTALS FOR THIS WEEK			

Average this week's total word count with the total page count. ....

Transfer Total Words and Total Pages to the **Foundations** page, which precedes this one.

Increasing counts create a sense of accomplishment and reveal the power of persistence.

Calculating Words and Pages to Session Time helps determine if you are focused.

Wk 1 :: Day 1 (1::1) ~ Pick your Idea

What idea is intriguing you?

Letting words flow onto the page without direction is seductive. How many times have you written scene after scene only to fail at constructing those scenes into a coherent whole? The story awakes, an unbroken egg. Use a plan to crack it.

Most writers keep a notebook filled with ideas. Browse through your previous ideas, and select whatever sparks more ideas. Don't pick what everyone else is doing. Pick what *you* want to write.

If you don't have an assortment of ideas, then jot down the idea that keeps lurking in the corners, popping into your head when you least expect it.

- o   Who is the focus?
- o   How do you see them?
- o   How do you *view* them? *Seeing* is surface; *viewing* is deeper, into the essence.
- o   What is their goal?
- o   What is their dilemma? A dilemma is a choice between two bad alternatives. You need to consider these alternatives. Know the reason that each alternative is a bad choice for your focus character. What catastrophe might occur?

Rapidly write your answers to the first four bullets, letting the words flow rapidly without corrections. Don't try for complete, grammatically correct sentences. Just let the words flow.

Don't scratch out or erase or delete what you have written. Whatever you don't want to use, just run a double line through it and flow on. About 75-100 words for each question should spark more ideas.

Puzzle over the dilemma question. While the dilemma may not become the story's central conflict, it should create insight into what matters most to the focus character.

I would handwrite these answers, but you can type them if handwriting gives you the cold chills. The computer creates a barrier between me and the story. I will back up to add in or delete or make corrections instead of letting the words flow. The editor side of my brain won't let go. While I am an extremely fast typist, I am much faster with handwriting, especially with gel ink on smooth paper. The creative side of my brain engages when I handwrite.

From your responses to the five questions above, create a jot list of ideas, just a few things to mull over or explore or research. Writing these down will focus your subconscious. We've all heard that the subconscious works while we sleep. Studies show that presenting your mind with a question before you sleep will usually lead to an answer upon waking.

Last thing, if you do not already have an ideas notebook, make one. You can use a plain wire notebook, a three-ring binder, a pretty journal or a field notebook, whatever you find workable. Record stray ideas, intriguing quotations, and the like.

My current Ideas Notebook is a little large because I've reduced what I carry daily. I now carry a much smaller notebook and transfer any ideas into the larger notebook before I start my writing for the day. Transferring the ideas actually engages my brain for writing. (And the smaller notebook works until I burn through half the pages because inspiration strikes for my current story.)

Estimate your word count and record it. If you were computer-based, you should have your word count with no problem.

WK 1 :: DAY 2 (1::2) ~ PICK YOUR STORY

Before you start developing your story, you need to understand your story's *genre*. Genre simply means category. Just as there are many different classifications for art media (ink, acrylic, oil, watercolor, crayon), writing has classifications upon classifications. First we distinguish between prose and poetry. In the world of prose, we then separate fiction and nonfiction.

Go into any bookstore, and you will see broad categories for the books. In most stores, the fiction and nonfiction sections are on different sides. Both broad categories then break into smaller genres. Fiction divides into Classics, Literary, Mystery, Speculative (science fiction and fantasy), Romance, Western, Youth (which for some reason is called "young adult"), and Children's. I know I've skipped some categories.

Children's is further divided by age/reading level. Classics is usually shelved by time period.

To take one broad genre, Mystery can be subdivided into Amateur Sleuth, Cozy, Crime, Historical, Noir (or Hard-boiled), Detective or Police Procedural, Suspense, and Thriller. Even so, all the books are shelved in the same section.

When you approach genre as a reader, you often don't think of the areas within the broad field. You just read what you like. You ask for "another dragon book" or "an FBI agent chasing a twisted serial killer" or a "beach read that will make me cry".

Writers need more clarity than readers. We need to know the rules of our genre and subgenre, usually so we can maintain most rules but break a few.

You may read articles that say genre writing is dead. They "said" that about mysteries. The word was given out after Arthur Conan Doyle wrote his last Sherlock Holmes. Then along came Dorothy L. Sayers and Agatha Christie, re-inventing in two different directions what Conan Doyle had done.

Write what you want to, not what someone else tells you to write.

First, determine your broad category of genre then discover your subgenre. You'll have to do research for this. Thank goodness the internet is handy and for once will have the answers. Search "types of mystery stories" or "genres in science fiction" or "categories of fantasy novels". If you already know that you like steampunk instead of urban fantasy, great. You're ready for the next step.

Discover the subgenre's parameters. What does steampunk (or insert your genre) include; what does it exclude?

What are the basic rules that define the genre? Which basic rules do you wish to maintain? Which rules might you decide to break?

Any research can be a time-sucker. Don't get sidetracked. Spend your time wisely, and print out what you find. Don't forget to record your word count.

1 :: 3 ~ PICK YOUR PROTAGONIST

A protagonist is the primary character facing the central conflict of the story. The protagonist will be in the story from beginning to end.

In William Shakespeare's *Tragedy of Julius Caesar*, Caesar dies in Act III; the play continues for two more acts. Caesar is not the protagonist. We could argue that Mark Antony, in addition to Brutus, is a protagonist in the play.

We can also argue about the protagonist in F. Scott Fitzgerald's *The Great Gatsby*. Gatsby doesn't immediately enter the story, and he dies before we reach the end. Nick Carraway is often called "merely a narrator", yet he is the one conflicted most about appearance vs. reality, Fitzgerald's central conflict.

As you work through these questions, you can choose to handwrite your answers or type them onto your computer, whether that be a laptop, tablet, smartphone, or other electronic notetaking software.

- **Name** and anything special about that name (such as its meaning or that it's a combination of grandmothers or he's named for his father's favorite baseball player)

- **Necessities of Appearance.** Consider the obvious as well as the not-obvious: speech habits, dialects or special fluencies, stance, walk, tics or nervous habits, manner of dress, and tokens, such as good-luck charms.

- **Purpose vs. Desire.** Most people have jobs, but a few have careers. Everyone has dreams, but only a few crave a particular dream.
  - Jobs often give us purpose, but some people are driven by a greater purpose. Firefighters and law enforcement officers are usually filled with the purpose of defending those around them. What drives your protagonist forward?
  - What does your protagonist desire? A desire is a dream yearned after or craved. For angsty stories, the purpose often prevents attainment of the desire.

- **Strength vs. Weakness**. Physical strength and weakness, mental strength and weakness, moral strength and weakness. Knowing these three sets gives you a deeper insight into character. If you become stumped, consider the 7 Vices (deadly sins) and the 7 Virtues (heavenly virtues).
  - After *Raiders of the Lost Ark* hit the movie theatres, everyone started giving easy fears and weaknesses to protagonists. Fear of snakes or heights was easy to write into a script or story. Be more intriguing than the obvious.

- **Secret Angst.** What is a past event that still haunts your protagonist? What will s/he not wish to be revealed to anyone? To what lengths will your protagonist go to keep that secret hidden?

- **3 H's.** We all want people that we can admire, especially in our central characters. Most readers identify in some way with the primary characters in a story and become frustrated when that character does something that the reader deplores. We also don't want characters without backbone. We might think the characters should take the easy route, but we're never happy with the story when they do so. In the books that we love, the primary characters wrestle with personal dilemmas and decide to be extraordinary rather than only remaining extra-ordinary.

  o How will your protagonist be **honorable**? Two examples that reveal honor are standing against others and choosing the ethical over the expedient.
  o How will your protagonist be **heroic**? Enduring suffering without calling on others and risking personal safety for others are heroic acts.
  o How will your protagonist be **humble**? While a character can be assured and strong, s/he should not be arrogant and snobbish.
  o What **horrific event** would repulse your protagonist?

In writing these answers, you may have had scenes pop into your head. Quickly sketch out those scenes. Don't lose them. Your novel is beginning to build itself.

Don't forget to record your word count. Today you should have gone over your planned goal.

1 :: 4 ~ PICK YOUR ANTAGONIST

Great antagonists often mirror elements of the protagonist: Sherlock against Moriarty, Frodo and Golem, Hamlet and Claudius, and Edgar and Edward in Shakespeare's *King Lear*.

Mirrors can be similar or complete opposites. Indiana Jones' rival in *Raiders of the Lost Ark* is a German archaeologist who had decided to serve the goals of Hitler's Nazism rather than find ancient artifacts to assist the modern world (especially the university at which Indy taught). Darth Vader faced the same choices that his son Luke Skywalker faced. Fanny and Mary Crawford in *Mansfield Park* are complete opposites in appearance, outlook, and morals, yet they have the same interests, future dreams, and desires which they pursue in completely different ways.

Antagonists should not be straw men, easily knocked down. Even if the viewpoint of the antagonist is never given in the story, the writer needs to understand that character's inner life.

New writers want to make their antagonists all-powerful. How can a protagonist ever defeat an omnipotent opponent? The writer resorts to a coincidence or a lucky chance. That weakens the protagonist. If you are writing a series like J.K. Rowling, in which your protagonist will mature and strengthen, then yes, you can use coincidence and luck in the early books of the series. However, more is needed for the ultimate defeat. Study the various parts of the final battle against Voldemort, Nagini, Beatrix Lestrange, and the other evil minions to discover how neither coincidence nor luck develop the climax.

We're looking at many of the same elements.

- **Name** and reason for it.

- **Necessities of Appearance.**

- **Purpose IS the Desire**.

- **Strength vs. Weakness.**

- **Secret Past.**

- **3 H's**. Some of the best antagonists also make you root for them, and we cry for their defeat: Heathcliff in the *Wuthering Heights* films (but never the book). The antagonists that make us cringe are the ones who have no barriers to what they will do in order to achieve their Desire: Moriarty in the new *Sherlock* series, the Joker in the *Batman* series.

  - **Honorable or Dishonorable? Explain.**
  - **Heroic**? The opposite is cowardly. How does the antagonist **manipulate** others rather than personally committing evil? When an antagonist does something heroic, the purpose is often for a long-term plan that is destructive.
  - An antagonist's **humility will be false**. Most often, the antagonist's self-centered will creates arrogance or a false modesty so cleverly masked that many cannot see the truth.
- What past action clearly exhibits the antagonist's choice to be **horrific**?

Don't forget to record your word count. Once again you should have exceeded the goal.

1 :: 5 ~ PICK YOUR THEME

Theme means truth. Some writers call the theme a "tagline", a quick sentence or two that encapsulates the entire story.

Themes are universal statements, true for all people in all times. They will guide your character development and your story development. Often, a great story has multiple truths to explore. These same truths can be in many different stories.

- Deception has unexpected consequences. ~ *Romeo and Juliet. Hamlet. Much Ado About Nothing.* All three plays by Shakespeare.
- Violence injures the innocent. ~ *Romeo and Juliet.*
- Simple pleasures are the greatest delight.
- "There is within us, and with sadness I have watched it in others, a knot of cruelty, borne by the streams of love." ~ "The Scarlet Ibis" by James Hurst

Classic subjects are good vs. evil or appearance vs. reality. Themes drive the subject in a particular direction. Turn the subject into a sentence, and you have a theme, whether you choose to state it or merely imply it in your novel.

- Deception vs. Truth = subject
- Deception is a deeply tangled knot that is difficult to unravel. = theme

Notice how the theme in the example above is creating motifs for a story: knot, deeply tangled, difficult to unravel. We can use these as symbols for tangled relationships and knotty events, secrets and lies to be unraveled.

In my book *Christmas with Death*, the theme is "Christmas is for miracles, merriment, and murder." In *The Key with Hearts*, the theme is "A convenient marriage inconveniently causes murder." The theme as tagline should hint at the story.

Writing a tagline seems easy. It's not. Deliberate over your choice of tagline. Virtually every element of your story should depend on this single sentence. Your wording can change and refine as characters and events develop; however, the basic theme should not.

You may spend thirty solid minutes constructing 10 simple words. It's time well spent. You will refer back to this tagline with every scene you write.

Record today's seemingly pitiful word count, then tally up the entire week and record it on the **Foundations** page. If you did every part, you should have accomplished much more than you anticipated.

WEEK 2 :: SKETCH YOUR STORY

COMPLETION CHART

DAY / DATE	FOCUS ~ BRIEF INFO	PAGE COUNT	WORD COUNT	SESSION TIME
1	INTRODUCE PROTAGONIST			
2	INTRODUCE ANTAGONIST			
3	INTRODUCE SETTING			
4	BACKGROUND /ORIGINS			
5	DEVELOP / RESOLVE			
6	CATCH-UP			
7				
	TOTALS FOR THIS WEEK			

Average this week's total word count with the total page count. ....

Transfer Total Words and Total Pages to the **Foundations** page, which precedes Week 1.

Increasing counts create a sense of accomplishment and reveal the power of persistence.

Calculating Words and Pages to Session Time helps determine if you are focused.

A Story Sketch catches the basic outlines for your first vision of the story.

Last week we dug out the story that you want to write. This week we pour the groundwork for your novel. Unlike the concrete block foundation for a house, however, any structural details that you add this week can always be changed.

The best sketches are quickly written, casting the major concepts for the novel, just as an artist will sketch the primary elements of a canvas.

A sketch should never be detailed and convoluted. When we become detailed, we become wedded to specific elements and are reluctant to change them. As story flows out of us in the organic drafting process, we can *and* should expect early elements to morph. Those elements will be fleshed out. They might be transposed with others. They might even be dropped completely. We won't know what will happen. In the midst of writing, with the creative muse bouncing on our shoulders, we will expand upon, flip around, and delete elements. The muse will guide us (and drive us, as it sometimes seems) in certain story directions. New characters may appear. Setting may change. Unforeseen conflicts may arise.

If we were bound lock-step to specific things happening at specific times in specific ways, we would not want to abandon those steps. We would try to force the story up the steps where we want it to go.

Should we do that, however, our muse will lose her bounciness. If we prevent the story flow too much, the muse becomes dammed. Story stagnates. We can't see our next steps for the slimy growth caused by an outline we're determined to follow. By letting the story flow, ideas cascading onto the page, we keep the river undammed and the novel progressing.

Remember this as you work through these Foundation tasks.

Remember this as you draft.

2 :: 1 ~ SKETCH YOUR PROTAGONIST'S INTRODUCTION

Last week we built your primary characters. This week we want to reveal them through events. In looking at strengths and purposes, desires and the 3 H's, how can you *show* one of these aspects through the action of your protagonist?

To see heroism or humility displayed is much more effective than a sermon telling us.

- *Tell* > John has a soft heart for dogs.
- *Show* > The muddy puppy wriggled with excitement when John knelt before her. He lifted her with one hand then tucked her against his chest. Wet paws stained his white shirt, but he touched his nose to the pup's when she lifted her head. Her tail beat a

steady drum against his ribs.

Once you have the element you wish to show, determine the setting.

- Where is your protagonist?
- When? (time of day/night, season, year)
- What does your protagonist see? Hear? Feel?
- What is the climate?
- How does your protagonist feel about this setting?
- What brought him here? An event?

What is the danger your protagonist will face in this scene? This is the opening of your novel. You should present your primary character's normal existence then build to the event that starts the conflict for the entire book, whether that event is directly related to the conflict or merely tangential, like a spark drifting away from a campfire.

- James Scott Bell says that, at crucial moments, all protagonists face a death of some type: physical (their own or someone dear to them), personal (of a relationship or a job that gives purpose), or psychological (of a long-held dream or hope).

Which type of death will occur in this opening scene?

In medias res (a Latin term meaning "in the middle of things") is the time-honored way of starting a novel. Rather than completely showing a character in his existence who only gradually becomes aware of a conflict, starting *in medias res* quickly presents the character in danger. His responses to that danger exhibit massive amounts of information to the reader.

In our example above, immediately after John picks up the puppy, something must happen to place him—or the puppy or the people around him—in danger of some sort.

- Is a note attached to the puppy's collar, a note intercepted because the puppy came to John instead of someone else?
- Does the puppy offer an opportunity for John to meet someone who will change the focus and direction of his life?
- Is it not mud but blood that covers the puppy's paws?

Your choice for the danger depends upon the genre (and subgenre) of the story that you are writing.

2 :: 2 ~ SKETCH YOUR ANTAGONIST'S INTRODUCTION

Bring your antagonist into the opening scene with your protagonist.

While the protagonist is the primary character *facing* the conflict, the antagonist is the **conflict-creator**.

- In Shakespeare's *Julius Caesar*, the antagonist for Brutus is his ideal of the Roman Republic, an ideal that has him falling for Cassius' manipulative comments that Caesar wants to become an emperor.
- In *Great Gatsby*, Daisy Buchanan represents the corrupt social rank that Nick Carraway had lusted after before he saw beneath the beautiful frothy plaster to the blood-colored flooring underneath, hinted at in Fitzgerald's description of the Buchanan's home, less than ten pages into the book.

Many novels often open with the antagonist, displaying his villainy. Only then is the protagonist introduced.

Many novels only hint at the antagonist. The conflict that begins rolling seems more elemental, like a force of nature, rather than specific to a person.

Many novels present an evil that seems to be the antagonist while the conflict-creator is actually within the protagonist (like Cassius seems to be the antagonist in *Julius Caesar* but the conflict is within Brutus).

And some novels give no hint of their direction except through symbolic imagery (like the heavily plastered ceiling and claret-colored rug of the Buchanan's drawing room in *The Great Gatsby*.

As you draft your novel, your antagonist may morph, becoming more like Brutus' internal ideal or a social rank that seems like an institution it is so ingrained. Or you may decide to fix upon an institution only to have a representative of it become the true antagonist.

Remember, we are sketching ideas. The draft will solidify them.

Looking at your work in **2 :: 1**, discover how the antagonist will come on-stage.

Is s/he drawn or lured into the scene?

Is your protagonist drawn or lured or impelled by an event or required by circumstance to become involved?

Will the reader know immediately which character is the antagonist? Or will you only hint at the truth? Or will you drop hints later for the revelation at the dark moment of the story or in the climactic scene?

2 :: 3 ~ SKETCH YOUR SETTING

Readers need to be grounded. They need to envision the specifics of setting. The writer's job is to present place and time and culture.

While you want the major elements of setting to remain fluid, you can become detailed with the setting of this introductory scene. Such details add depth and richness to our writing.

Describe the setting of this first situation. Be specific. Don't just say "house". Describe the kind of house, the color of the siding and the roof. If you have a house with brown brick rather than red, let the reader see brown by describing it as "earth-shaded brick".

What would the characters hear? What creates the sounds? What is the distance of those sounds from the characters? On a busy street you will have a cacophony of sounds. In a suburb, you will still have multiple sounds, from vehicles on distant roads to birds chirping to dogs barking in a neighbor's house.

What would the characters feel? The cold from air conditioning? The wind cooling their skin on a hot summer day? The stickiness of the tape used for binding wounds? Can what the characters feel be related to their jobs or their purpose?

How can smell be a factor? Noxious and penetrating smells are easier to describe, but sweet smells can create a juxtaposition with the danger occurring.

Ground your readers by writing about 350 words to describe your setting. Determine the best places in your work for **2 :: 1** and **2 :: 2** to use these details.

2 :: 4 ~ SKETCH YOUR BACKGROUND

Background is essential to the writer, but readers may never see it. Most of the background and the research that you will do for any story will never be displayed to your audience. It *informs* you as you write the novel.

You have to know some of the background before you begin the draft. Consider as background the details that you make up about characters and places in your book. *Research*, however, is factual information about the real world.

Whatever you do, don't *info dump*.

The best definition of *info dump* is information regurgitated onto the novel's page without necessity for character or scene or event. For example, in an alien-invasion science fiction novel, 300 words describing the development of the first space probe that left our solar system (which lured the aliens here) would be straight *info dump*. Use that information sparingly, if at all.

Researched information should be seeded in, snippets at a time. Name a character for the man whose greeting to space occurs first on the Voyager I program that developed the probe. Then, as he works on a solution to fight the aliens, someone can point out, "Hey, you're Kurt Waldheim? Isn't that the name of the man who recorded the greeting to aliens for the Voyager I probe?"

John D. MacDonald included a lot of factual research about sailing in his novels, especially the Travis McGee books. The information pops onto the page in snippets rather than in whole spates of info dump.

As you draft the novel, you will discover that you need even more research or background. You can choose to pursue this information at that time (and break the flow of the novel) or merely make a note and wait for revision. During revision, you may discover additional information is needed. In this age of the computer, it is simple to add information into previous locations of a document.

The background you need now is this:

- How did the introductory situation develop? Know its origin up to the entrance of the primary characters.

2 :: 5 ~ SKETCH YOUR DIRECTION

Before you call the writing for a day finished, you need to know where the story is heading.

Every time you finish a scene—especially if you are a puzzler, jumping around to write different scenes—you need to jot down your ideas for the event that will develop next.

In **2 :: 4**, you discovered how the opening situation developed. You know the basics of your two primaries, and ideas should be percolating for the next scenes in the book.

A jot list for your next direction will provide not only details about the upcoming scene but also the reason for those details. Even if you plan to write the very next day—or later in the afternoon or the evening, something might happen to disrupt your plans.

The jot list helps you pick back up.

You can always abandon the jot list or save it for a later scene. Beginning writers, especially, plan the next scene only for the subconscious to work on their writing problems while they sleep. They may rewind several scenes or jump ahead to a later scene and become involved in those later scenes.

Anything can happen to delay your return to this point of the book. Including life.

So, here's what to include in your jot list. Remember, this is a sketch, broad outlines only.

If you think of great dialogue, use a sticky note (an essential writer's tool).

- How will the opening situation resolve?
- Is the protagonist and/or the antagonist involved in that resolution?
- Who helped the situation develop?
- Did the situation morph beyond its expected development?
- Who else helped with the resolution of the opening situation?
- Which characters have entered the story?
- What will happen next?

At this point, I like to print everything out. I'm a tactile, visual person who likes goal completion. Having something visible in my hands is a much better incentive for a long-term goal like novel publication. Having manuscript pages and background notes out on my desk is a constant reminder of a task I wish to complete.

Organize your Electronic Files

If you have not yet done so, in your File Explorer (the gathering place of your computer's files), create a specific file for this manuscript. Name it a short version of your title. Slide everything into that file. All your generated documents, from story development, to character documents, to research and background.

If you've been putting everything in one document, break it out into separate documents: you have your novel file, research files (I would keep these as separate documents), character development and background files (also separate). Later, you will add your converted publishing files and cover images files.

Creating the single folder enables an easy search for materials months and years from now.

Years? Yes, years. You're in this for the long haul, right? In a handful of years, you might decide to turn this book into a series.

THE MASTER BOOK FOR YOUR BOOK

By now, you should have noticed that you are starting to "see" elements of your primary characters' appearance as well as setting. You should see new characters entering your novel. Now is the time to create a Master Book which lists the specific details for all primary, secondary, and tertiary characters (the walk-ons who might just show up in a later scene or a later book).

At this point, you have no idea who will show up in Chapter 15. Jot down the info so you don't have to look for it later. You have no idea if you will need the name of the imaginary subway stop in Chapter 11, but it's in the notes when you do need it.

Some writers also find stock images for characters and setting.

You can put this information in another electronic document in your folder for this novel, or you can create a print journal specific for this novel. Or you can use a ring binder.

All sorts of snippets go in the Master Book. Some call it the "Bible" because it sets up and allows you to follow strict guidelines that prevent errors that readers will notice and comment on.

Whatever type of "holder" you create, you need to be able to pick it up and find what you're looking for very quickly.

For my Regency Mysteries, since I have so many different connections, I have genealogical charts that I've created as well as house plans that I've drawn, menus for dinners, seating arrangements for dinners, a taped-in chart of British titles and addresses in ascendancy, Basque and Spanish terms (for *The Key for Spies*), and lists of red herrings and clues to the murderer with chapter and page numbers. And much more.

For my *Into Death* series, I originally considered the first book as a one-off and didn't create a Master Book. When ideas for the second book began developing, I had to go back through the first novel and make the necessary notes.

Having learned my lesson, I now create a Master Book every time I start a novel. For a series, the Master pages all go into the same binder, easily accessible. I have a mass Master that contains several one-offs.

WEEK 3 :: KNOW YOUR STORY ~ A

COMPLETION CHART

DAY/ DATE	SUMMARY	PAGE COUNT	WORD COUNT	SESSION TIME
1	BEGIN			
2	A DEAR DESIRE			
3	END			
4	STRESS POINT			
5	NADIR			
6				
7				
	TOTALS FOR THIS WEEK			

Average this week's total word count with the total page count. ....

Transfer Total Words and Total Pages to the **Foundations** page, which precedes Week 1.

Increasing counts create a sense of accomplishment and reveal the power of persistence.

Calculating Words and Pages to Session Time helps determine if you are focused.

3 :: 1 ~ BEGIN

For the next two weeks, we start the novel, writing ten scenes around which everything will pivot. These ten scenes are the Plot 7.

With the Foundational understanding of protagonist and antagonist, you can develop the necessary scenes that are the main points on the arc of the story. Plot 7 represents the pivotal scenes.

You *could* continue to play at writing, filling out templates and sketching out ideas here and there. Play without purpose, however, does not achieve the goal of publication.

Writing Goal :: Begin

Time to write the full-blown introductory scene where the protagonist meets the antagonist.

Flesh out last week's sketch introducing the protagonist and antagonist. Add details as you go: details of character opinion—of self, of other characters, of the situation. Write the descriptive details of the setting and the situation. Touch on the strong identifiers only as you describe the primary characters.

Unfold your protagonist's realization of the primary conflict, whether by hint or actual statement. Depending on your genre and your own wishes, you do not have to point the finger at the specific antagonist. Indeed, misidentification is a time-honored method of adding suspense to any book.

The antagonist does not have to be *identified* in the role as conflict-creator. Many novelists do introduce the antagonist as such very early on, often before the protagonist is introduced. Nevertheless, a good mystery rule to follow, whether your genre is mystery or fantasy or military thriller, is to introduce the antagonist *on the page* before the end of the first chapter. You need not identify the antagonist as such.

The antagonist's introduction must hint at being the true conflict-creator, neither ally nor a neutral character. Name known or unknown, glee revealed or hidden, the antagonist drives the story forward.

That's an important point. For the first part of your novel, the antagonist acts while the protagonist reacts. By the last third, your protagonist should be acting while the antagonist is reacting. This guideline holds *unless* you're writing literary fiction. Protagonists aren't successful in literary fiction.

By the time you finish today's writing session, you may have hints at the antagonist's unveiling. Make notes of those hints.

You may wish to have the protagonist's realization of the conflict unfold over several events of the story: make notes of how that unfolding will occur. The first step of that realization, for the protagonist and the reader, needs to occur here in the opening of the book.

And the evil performed by the antagonist ***must*** *be known* before the first chapter is completed. Revealing the perpetrator of this evil may be delayed until the novel's very end.

3 RULES FOR WRITING

1. **Honor the Muse**. Write as clean a draft as you can. "Clean drafts" do not leave holes in the story. Don't think "I can always revise later". Do think "I will figure this out now." Weeks from now, you may decide to change scenes, increasing suspense or adding/subtracting characters, or shifting the flow of information. This is perfectly fine to do. Having something written already makes the later fixes easier.

2. **Pay the Piper**. Don't skip the hard parts. If you get stuck, write the next sentence and then the next. Truly stuck? Take a brief respite from the computer. As soon as you return, start writing immediately. Ignore the distractions. During that respite, don't pick up your smartphone. Don't plant yourself in front of the TV. Ignore phone calls. (Calls can go to voice mail. Yes, that's perfectly all right to do.)

3. **Stay Healthy.** Obey the 30/5 or the 45/15 breaks. For every 30 minutes of writing (or 45 minutes), take a 5-minute (or 15-minute) break. These breaks will re-charge your creativity. During your break, walk away from all electronics. Move around. The brain is dependent upon circulation. Drink water—purified or spring, without additions that contain sugar. Don't snack. Writing time is not the time for eating; eating time is meal time.

3 MATH EQUATIONS FOR WRITING

How much will you write? That's hard to dictate. Different stories demand different opening scenes. Different writers will always have different word counts.

A manuscript generally has 285 words per page (wpp). Page estimates are for a standard font at 12, with one-inch page margins, and range from 250 to 300 words. Variations occur for denser descriptive pages and for heavy dialogue pages.

To complete the NaNoWriMo challenge—50,000 words in 30 days—writers average 1,666 words per day (wpd).

E 1 :: 285 **wpp** with 1,666 **wpd** will result in about 6 pages per day. Choose a page-count or a word-count goal. I record both in my planner. You should do likewise until you know what works for you. Once you reach around 150 pages of the manuscript, you can test your own **wpp** against your **wpd**.

E 2 :: At 150 pages in, you should also determine your average pages per scene and average pages per chapter. You should see a working system developing. Once your personal system develops, you can project how long a novel may take to write.

E 3 :: In the early days of writing, more time is needed to achieve the daily goal. The more often that you write, the more rapidly will come the words that you write. The more you allow the creative muse to flow, turning off the critical editor, the less time you will need to achieve that daily goal. When you hit the rate of about 1,000 words per hour, you're working at the Pro Writer rate.

3 :: 2 ~ A DEAR DESIRE

William Shakespeare is a master of pacing. Most high school students who slogged through his plays will disagree with that statement. However, watch the better films for *Hamlet* and *Macbeth* and *Romeo and Juliet* and *King Lear*, *Much Ado about Nothing* and *Midsummer Night's Dream*. You are soon caught up in the story.

Then watch the film again, following along with the text. One thing you quickly notice is that Shakespeare spends an inordinate amount of time developing Acts I & II & III. Act IV runs half the length of the preceding act. Act V closes very quickly.

Acts I and II are the longest because they have so much to set up: primary characters and conflict, situation and themes, foreshadowing and setting.

All novels are similar. The opening scenes are much longer than the concluding scenes.

For **3 :: 1** you introduced the opening event that crystallizes the conflict for the protagonist. You have both primary characters on stage—although the antagonist in that role may still be hidden.

Now we twist the knife a little deeper for the protagonist—because readers love angst, and every writer begins as a reader.

We need to destroy the dear desire of the protagonist. Whether the desire is an actual person or a thing (from a job promotion to the hiding of a destructive secret) or a place (a symbol of the protagonist's family or the embodiment of a dream), we have to destroy it. The threat alone is not enough.

This destruction is the only thing that will set the protagonist moving on the hard journey that will transform her/him. No one wants to change. Only sacrifice will drive us through it.

The destruction may be literal or figurative. The antagonist will not be able to resist the destruction of this dear desire, and that irresistibility will reveal the antagonist's evil heart and the protagonist's protective heart.

If you work this scene through the Interrogatory 7—*who, what, where, when, how, why*—you will reach *by whose aid*. The sacrifice needs to be important to the protagonist and one other person. This increases the need for the protagonist to start the difficult and transformative journey to defeat the antagonist.

By whose aid also includes the person assisting the antagonist. You might sacrifice this person at this point, causing the protagonist to believe the conflict is over, or sacrifice them later into the story only to reveal the person as an assistant or minion to the antagonist, an unanticipated and greater evil.

Writing Goal :: Destroy the Dear Desire

Sketch out the answers to the Interrogatory 7, from *who* to both sides of the *by whose aid*.

Weave those answers into the writing you did yesterday, first setting up the dear desire then gradually creating it as the focus of the destruction, and finally destroying it.

You're not finished, though. You need to present the protagonist's first and devastated reaction to its destruction.

Destruction of the Dear Desire here at the opening of the novel does one major thing for your reader: it ratchets up the suspense level. While the reader will consciously think you will not destroy the protagonist, the reader's subconscious will persist in believing that you will.

And here's something for your own subconscious to mull over: this Dear Desire will be discovered as only an illusion for the protagonist. An actual and attainable Dear Desire will present itself deeper into the story. The protagonist will achieve this Dear Desire—only to have it threatened by the antagonist.

And when this second, more powerful Dear Desire is placed in danger, the reader's suspense level is screwed tighter and tighter.

Oh, the thrill of the angst!

3 :: 3 ~ END

The Beginning and the Dear Desire form the opening stage of the Plot 7.

Today, we focus on Stage 2, the End of the Novel.

It's seems counter-productive to write an end as we start the beginning.

Everything we write drives toward the end. As his second of seven highly effective habits, Stephen Covey said, "Begin with the end in mind."

Novel writing is the same way. Once we know the end, we write toward it. Everything we add—all the twists and motifs, all the characters and settings, all the thematic elements and suspenseful clues—all works toward the end.

The end is not the ultimate face-off between the protagonist and the antagonist. It is the ultimate, unspoken goal of the protagonist.

Harry Potter's greatest desire was to belong. At the end of the series, he belongs to an elite group that keeps all wizards safe. He is surrounded by his friends and his family. He successfully launches his son into a world which he knows his son will love and in which he also knows his son will remain safe.

Writing Goal :: The Paradise of the End

Here are the basic questions you need to answer. Sketch your ideas quickly then write the scene.

- What kind of ending do you want: tragic, happy, melancholic, thrilling? What impression will your readers have when they close the book?
- How do you want the protagonist to end up? In what physical / intellectual / emotional state?
- How does the protagonist react when s/he has the new dear desire in "hand"?
- How will the reader know that the protagonist has triumphed over evil? Even in a series, the protagonist has to triumph at the end of each novel. Why does a reader keep reading? Because a well-liked protagonist has won once and will need to win again.

This ending is the one that will most likely change more than any other of these foundational scenes.

Endings begin at the beginning.

They often wrap back to elements that you added to your beginning, whether those elements developed characters or setting.

Often, writers return the ending to a pivotal early setting, just as J.K. Rowling returned Harry to the station where everyone boards the train for Hogwarts. This time-honored method book-ends or *frames* the novel, creating a sense of completion.

Readers want to close the book with a good feeling. I've heard professional writers say that the opening sentence sells the first book; the ending sells the next book. Satisfy the reader, and sell the next book.

Finally, be aware that your endings will very likely present to the world what is most important in your own life.

We writers bleed our hopes and dreams and fears and hates onto the page. Critiques that analyze a writer's body of work often discover the person behind the stories. And that's okay.

3 :: 4 ~ STRESS POINT

Plot 3 of the 7 is your preliminary view of the protagonist's greatest stress point.

We're jumping around, building strong scenes. When we finish the Plot 7, you will have the skeleton of your novel intact. You will still need to add the organs and circulatory system and flesh that makes it a complete body of work. When you consider the final result, this skeleton should give you delight.

What event will put the protagonist in extreme stress? All three elements of the individual must come into play in this scene. Physical stress is easy to write. Intellectual stress? Not so much.

How do we write intellectual stress? We place a dilemma before the protagonist. A dilemma, as discovered in **1 :: 1**, is a choice between two bad alternatives, a choice between evils.

Intellectual stress would place the protagonist in a situation similar to one that the antagonist has created. You may wish to mimic the opening evil, and the protagonist discovers the choices will result in the same destruction that the antagonist wrought.

Return to your ideas originally developed at **1 :: 1**. Often, our early ideas only need a little sharpening to become the sticky point on which everything will pivot.

Emotional stress is the third element that we writers must wring out of the protagonist. When the intellectual dilemma is tied to emotional stressors, you have achieved strong angst.

Writing Goal :: Stressors for the Stress Point

What will be the protagonist's emotions during this Stress Point?

When s/he knows the antagonist is gloating, how will s/he react? How will s/he recover from the Stress Point?

And how will the protagonist's reactions be diametrically opposed to the antagonist's reactions in the same situation?

Here is another opportunity to wrap the novel. As **3 :: 3** wrapped from end to beginning, this scene should wrap from the three-quarters point to the ultimate battle. These chain links bind up the reader's satisfaction level.

Enrich this scene with the protagonist's emotions, adding enough to contrast them with the physical evidence of your antagonist's emotions when you're writing the climax.

3 :: 5 ~ NADIR

The nadir is the lowest point of the celestial sphere, according to astronomy. In writing, the high point of the story is not the climax. It is the zenith, the point at which the protagonist feels the greatest power, emotional soaring, intellectual success, and/or physical prowess.

The nadir is the opposite of each of those. It is the lowest and most unsuccessful point in a story. In the Archetypal Story Pattern (ASP), this is the Ordeal. Other story structures call this the Dark Moment.

It is the cave from which no return seems possible. The protagonist is so deep into the cave that no light from above penetrates and nothing gives guidance for any exit.

Writing Goal :: The Dark Nadir

What event will place the protagonist into the nadir?

As you did with the Stress Point, **3 :: 4**, develop the physical, intellectual and emotional sides of the protagonist. Track each through the fall into the nadir, the wallowing in the misery of it, and then the climb from it as the protagonist discovers the solution to escaping *and* defeating the antagonist.

This is the antagonist's greatest triumphal moment. The triumph s/he feels should contrast starkly with the protagonist's emotions. The antagonist has prevented the protagonist from achieving the new Dear Desire. (Remember **3 :: 2**?) How does the antagonist react?

Before you go any further, make notes of how this solution can be foreshadowed or developed. Magical skills do not automatically appear. Physical skills must be developed. Intellectual creativity breaks the walls of hide-bound tradition first. Decide how you will plant the developing skills. How can you foreshadow the solution?

And remember that foreshadowing remains in the **shadows**. The official definition says *hints and clues of what is to come*. Hints and clues are only seen by people in hindsight, as they look back. You will need to slide these clues in as stage whispers, stronger than actual whispers but unheard by the other characters and your readers.

Evil chuckles may occur as you finish this scene. Tears may result. Beg forgiveness. And give the muse time off for cleansing and re-charging.

NOTES OF THE WORK TO COME

Before you leave this week, you should have accumulated several structural notes.

In **3 :: 1**, you noted down how the antagonist will be unveiled throughout the book.

If the protagonist misidentified the antagonist, you have notes about where the misidentification itself will be unveiled, also from the first day.

You also made notes about the protagonist's understanding of the unfolding conflict.

Look at **3 :: 2** for ideas about the first Dear Desire becoming illusory. These notes will help exhibit the true Dear Desire being recognized by the protagonist.

In **3 :: 3** you picked up a few ideas about elements that create the idyllic world restored to the protagonist. Create at least three notes about the two strongest of these elements.

And from **3 :: 5**, pull the notes about the protagonist's necessary development of skills that will lead to the solution. Keep the skills essential to but NOT predictive of the solution. Discard your first couple of ideas; go with the third, fourth, fifth, and following ones.

Now, with all these notes gathered up, put them into some kind of order. This week is like skeletal bones scattered around. You can lay them in an order, but they lack necessary connections.

Those connectors are coming.

In looking back at the novel you're starting, are you happy with your production? Does the project still seem overwhelming? Are you seeing the pieces coming together so that you have an idea of the jigsawed novel?

With half the skeleton in place, are more ideas flowing, giving you opportunity for malicious chuckles as well as heart-filled joy? Judge as a writer.

As I noted previously, I'm visual. I tack everything to a large art board at this point. Finished scenes go at their appropriate places. Tacked notes give me reminders when I'm ready to tackle those scenes. I can stand back and see the story come together.

If you're working on computer, you can create an outline chart, but it's not the same as a physical chart. Software for writing, such as *Scrivener*, is supposed to provide a tack board that helps you see what's to come. When my computer is off, though, I don't see those things.

The tack board keeps me focused on my goal. You're three weeks into your goal of publishing. How many words have you written? How many pages?

What will keep you focused on the long-term goal? That focus is all that really matters.

WEEK 4 :: KNOW YOUR STORY ~ B

COMPLETION CHART

DAY/ DATE	SUMMARY	PAGE COUNT	WORD COUNT	SESSION TIME
1	ZENITH			
2	EARLY EVIL WIN			
3	FINAL BATTLE			
4	EARLY TWIST			
5	BETRAYAL			
6				
7				
	TOTALS FOR THIS WEEK			

Average this week's total word count with the total page count. …………………..

Transfer Total Words and Total Pages to the **Foundations** page, which precedes Week 1.

Increasing counts create a sense of accomplishment and reveal the power of persistence.

Calculating Words and Pages to Session Time helps determine if you are focused.

4 :: 1 ~ ZENITH

We ended the previous week at the protagonist's lowest point. As the novel grows into a complete body—bones, organs, connective tissue, and flesh—you may discover additional ways to wring the greatest angst from the Nadir.

Whatever changes you make, never *delete*.

You may decide to use the cut information at another point or in a different book. Keep everything, just remove it from this novel. Place it into an ideas file, either in the folder for this book or in a miscellaneous folder in File Explorer.

We start this week with a happier stage of the novel: the **Zenith**. As the nadir is the lowest point in the celestial sphere of astronomy, the zenith is the highest point of the sun (or any star) in the sky, directly opposed to the nadir.

In the novel's Zenith, the protagonist feels the greatest potential for success. Emotions soar. Ideas succeed. Strength triumphs. Evil is defeated.

Place this scene after the Stress Point, **3 :: 4**, after the Nadir, or after one of the later tribulations that the protagonist still has to face. This Zenith forms part of that tribulatory scene. Since it could potentially follow **4 :: 4** or **4 :: 5**, why are we writing the Zenith now? Why not wait?

Part of the reason, not the greatest, is that the muse needs a bit of joy after the Stress Point and the Nadir. The muse needs to see happiness before tackling the Final Battle, an Early Twist, and a Betrayal.

These five scenes, from Stress Point to Betrayal, are usually where our creative impulses bog down. We might slog through them. If our characters only have hardship to anticipate, if no hope is in the offing, then the entire novel process seems hopeless. Creativity slows until it achieves a snail pace. Once that happens, we either ditch the entire manuscript for something more exciting or we inch along, never quite achieving anything.

Give the muse hope with the Zenith.

Here's the greatest reason to write the Zenith at this point. The snippets of descriptors and character opinion and situational elements that form the Zenith will leak into the tribulatory scenes, creating strong juxtaposition. Readers may not consciously see that dynamic juxtaposition of high with low or good against evil, but their subconscious will see it.

Subconscious notes that link up will create reader satisfaction. Please the reader, and sell the next book.

So, while **4 :: 1** is a separate day, today's writing will be attached at the back end of a tribulation, dragging the protagonist and the reader out of the morass of depressive sorrow.

Writing Goal :: Joy for the Zenith

At what does the protagonist succeed? How is the task difficult or complex? How can *only* this protagonist achieve the task?

How did the protagonist develop the idea for the successful completion of the task? What cued her/him in to the solution? What difficulties occurred with the solution? How was each difficulty overcome?

What strengths did the protagonist need? Strength can be physical or mental, related to endurance or stamina, concentrated on an individual's ability to think creatively or juggle multiple thought processes simultaneously. Emotional strength is necessary to climb out of a pit; weak people refuse to climb and wallow in misery.

Trauma is different from weakness. Past traumas can be debilitating. If your protagonist has faced trauma, how does s/he overcome it? What builds this strength?

A problem's complexity and intricacy exhibit the protagonist's intellect in solving it. Brute force is something that any character could have achieved. Add force to intricacy, and you come closer to the protagonist as the only person who could think up the solution.

What soaring emotions will the protagonist feel? How will those emotions be expressed?

How are the antagonist and minions defeated? Where is the protagonist in situation and setting after their defeat? Where are the evil people? How do they discover the protagonist succeeded, and what is their reaction?

Structure Goals

Time for more notes. Look over what you've written.

- Where do you need to foreshadow?
- What specific symbolic motifs developed that you now want to work into the tribulatory scenes?
- Who did you introduce in this scene? Slot their introduction into your notes. Put a couple of sticky notes (physical or electronic) to remind yourself to write them into other scenes.
- If you worked with the protagonist's trauma, locate other places where you will mention the trauma. Use the trauma as a weakness in an early scene. How will the protagonist find the strength to overcome this weakness? Note that as well.

4 :: 2 ~ EARLY EVIL WIN

This scene sets up the Stress Point at **3 :: 4**. While several scenes will intervene, the Early Evil Win with the Stress Point start stacking the odds against the protagonist.

Stacking the odds builds your protagonist into a heroic character who overcomes multiple obstacles. Readers often identify with the protagonists in novels and films. Give them a protagonist who exhibits noble thoughts and behaviors. Like the Sam Neill character in *Jurassic Park I* and *III*, the protagonist should behave honorably and heroically. Sacrifice of life is not necessary to display honor and heroism. Doing the right thing, doing the difficult thing, doing what's best in the long-term will display those characteristics.

On the other hand, the antagonist needs to be dishonorable, cheating a way to success. Short-term goals that care nothing about long-term consequences develop an egocentric attitude.

With this Early Evil Win, contrast the antagonist and the protagonist in their ethics, willingness to sacrifice for others, and focus on goals that are short-term versus long-term.

Writing Goal :: Evil Wins but Lacks Morals

In the Early Evil Win, the antagonist either defeats the protagonist or creates a successful obstacle that prevents the protagonist from achieving a long-term goal. What occurs?

How does the protagonist react?

How does the antagonist react?

Where will the protagonist go from here? Remember, in this early part of the novel, the protagonist is reactive. S/he does not know the antagonist's next step but will fear it. A full realization of the antagonist is still to come, but the shadows of that realization have grown darker, more fully silhouetted.

What does the antagonist plan next?

Structure Goals

Look for ways to foreshadow the Early Evil Win. Also note times when both the protagonist and the antagonist look back on this Early Win with their contrasting opinions as they are going forward in the story.

4 :: 3 ~ FINAL BATTLE

The Final Battle is the ultimate show-down between the protagonist and the antagonist. At the end of the Final Battle, the antagonist is completely defeated.

If you're writing a series, you may have a master antagonist as well as specific antagonists for each book. The master antagonist will only be defeated in the final book. The specific antagonist for each book must be defeated—otherwise, you are writing a series of cliffhangers. Most readers don't appreciate cliffhangers unless they can read all the books of the series in a binge weekend.

The Final Battle should place the protagonist in the greatest jeopardy. The stakes are high in this scene. One or the other of the two primary characters will die, whether the death is physical, personal, or professional.

The antagonist should fully expect to win. Minions are in place. The odds seem stacked in the antagonist's favor.

The protagonist will have allies. Even though the odds seem stacked, they are not. The protagonist has the winning ace. Harry knew that Voldemort's wand wouldn't really work for him. Frodo had Sam Gamgee. While these are quest/action-adventure, the story structure is clearly revealed in such novels and films. The scenes are built just the same as in other genres of fiction.

The ace in the final *Godfather* film is the nephew who will inherit the role. The death of his love, the sinister evil he has partaken of, all structure him as a more ruthless Godfather than any before.

Consider the Final Battle scenes in other books and films. Look for the ace that will help the protagonist succeed. All of them are there.

None of them are coincidence, luck, happenstance.

Writing Goal ~ Take Down!

What sets up this final encounter?

Describe the setting. Make it come alive. This is the climactic scene of the entire novel. Readers should see it, hear it, smell it, feel it physically and emotionally.

What are the deadly consequences? How do both the protagonist and the antagonist understand these consequences? How does this understanding of consequences affect each of them?

How will you show that the antagonist expects to win? Gloating? Sneering? How do the minions behave?

What special skills has the protagonist learned or acquired that defeats the antagonist?

What occurs in the Final Battle? What will the allies and the minions do? One of the interesting side notes in the last Harry Potter are the evil minions who are fleeing the battle. (Harry's weak allies fled before this battle. The strong ones remained.)

What will the antagonist do at the end of the Final Battle? How will the surviving minions behave?

What will the protagonist do at the end of the Final Battle?

Structure Goals

- Are you seeing additional characters come onto stage? They will need specific descriptive identifiers, either for behavior or appearance.
- These characters have to be introduced much earlier in the book.
- Anyone actively used in the Final Battle must appear in one other scene. Consider the number of times that Beatrix Lestrange and Draco Malfoy's father appeared. Twice before the Final Battle is acceptable. Three is considered the charmed number.
- Any ace also needs its separate introduction and use.
- Note down the two-plus times that the special skill to defeat the antagonist is learned or acquired. Success does not usually happen immediately. Perhaps the protagonist can try out the skill only to fail. Practice is necessary. How many times will the protagonist practice? How many times will the protagonist fail? The incidences of failure must lessen as you approach the novel's Final Battle. Otherwise, the success will seem like coincidence, which is not acceptable as a solution for readers.

4 :: 4 ~ Early Twist

Great writers know how to keep readers guessing, whether that speculation is related to character development or plot structure.

The Early Twist scene adds irony to your novel.

Irony is the difference between what readers will expect to happen versus what will actually happen, otherwise known as situational irony. Another way to look at irony is the difference between what appears to be versus what actually is (classic irony)

In Situational Irony, something will happen, and the crushing ball will tilt in the opposite direction from what was expected.

In Classic Irony, a character can appear to be one way but is actually another.

Writing Goals ~ Choose a Twist

To twist your protagonist, you can write a scene where the protagonist expects an event that will be helpful to her/him.

- What is the expectation that the protagonist wants to exult over?
- How does that expectation change?
- How is that expectation's change foreshadowed? (Yep, foreshadowing necessary. You will need to blind the protagonist as well as the reader.)

This is not a surprising, completely unexpected event. It can be a shock, but you need to have planned for its occurrence. Remember: shun the appearance of coincidence.

To twist a character, you can have that person seem to be on the side of the protagonist—but not be (save this one for the Betrayal, upcoming). Or you can have that person appear to be on the side of the antagonist but actually is not. Choose this one.

One of the more memorable characters in a recent novel is one that appeared to be employed by a minion of the antagonist. She was trapped because the minion had evidence that he threatened to use against her brother (who she had raised after their parents died). When she finally located and removed the evidence entangling her brother, she also collected more evidence against the minion. This also contained evidence against the antagonist—a neat ace for the protagonist. She presented all of this to the protagonist. Suspicious at first, the protagonist neglected looking at the full evidence until later in the novel.

You always want more than one twist in a novel.

You can write both of these scene choices. This is your novel; you can do what you want.

For additional guidance, look at the questions for the Early Evil Win. Remember to write the protagonist's shock at the outcome.

Structure Goals

Remember to make notes to foreshadow that the situational irony will not fall in the direction that the protagonist anticipates.

For the classic irony with a character, the notes you make can be as simple as taking a phone call overheard by the protagonist that sets up the importance of a relationship and the character's background and goals.

4 :: 5 ~ BETRAYAL

One of the most painful experiences that anyone has is Betrayal. This is more than a promise not fulfilled. Betrayal hits everyone in the gut.

The scene for Betrayal will usually occur before the Stress Point or before the Final Battle. Someone that the protagonist depended upon greatly flees just when they are most needed.

Study the meaning of the word *betrayal*. It is not disloyalty. Or broken promises. Or infidelity or unfaithfulness. It is treachery. It is as deep as a heart stabbed from behind when the protagonist expected a hug.[1]

Betrayal takes away hope. Of the 7 scenes in the Plot 7, this may be the most important emotional one. Don't skimp on it.

Writing Goal ~ Stab the Heart

Who does the protagonist believe is a match in personal goals and wishes, hopes and dreams?

How will that character betray the protagonist?

Why will that character betray her/him? This is the most important question. When the betrayal is discovered, the character will try to justify it. No justification is acceptable, but actions can be mitigated.

The reason that no justification is acceptable is that an ultimate sacrifice resulted from the betrayal. Who will die? Remember, death can be physical, personal, or professional—but physical death is the strongest. How will this death affect the protagonist? How will the death create a huge hole in the protagonist's heart?

After the early loss of the illusory dear desire, **3 :: 2**, the death caused by this betrayal will make the protagonist question everything.

When the lost person, the one who dies, had the protagonist's goal as their own, then achieving that goal becomes doubly important to the protagonist.

The betrayal will cause the antagonist to gloat—but the antagonist will lack the protagonist's emotional depth. The antagonist could care less about the person who dies. They are merely removed from the chess board, never to return.

Structure Goals

You now have an additional character that you will need to weave into the earlier scenes of the story. This character needs to be sympathetic to the readers (not too much so, or everyone will automatically guess—correctly—that they will die. Remember the importance of surprise.).

---

[1] This paragraph originally occurred in *Think like a Pro: New Advent for Writers*, book one of this series.

You also have an additional character to introduce. The traitor can be sympathetic or not. Whether you choose to redeem the traitor by having him sacrifice himself for the goal is your choice. (Remember Boromir in *The Fellowship of the Ring*?)

Knowing the traitor's reason for the betrayal is crucial.

If the betrayal occurs because the traitor is loyal to the antagonist and lied to the protagonist, then you will need to write the antagonist giving instructions to the traitor. This creates dramatic irony, where the audience knows information that the protagonist does not. When you have dramatic irony occur without a dire result followed by a scene where the dire result *does* occur, you have successfully outwitted the reader, who expects the betrayal but not yet.

Finally, you need to make notes about the protagonist's confrontation with the traitor, when the traitor attempts to justify an unjustifiable action. The protagonist cannot just forgive the traitor, even when the reasons for the betrayal were completely understandable. Betrayal removes all trust. This character will now lurk far on the sidelines of the novel.

If the traitor feels guilt, they can become involved again as the ace in the Final Battle. Or they can provide the ace, having searched for it as a means to redeem themselves.

If the traitor feels no guilt, then they need to be shown once more in the antagonist's direct employ. And if the antagonist doesn't trust them, that's reality.

Do you want them to receive justice for their actions? Should they? What will the readers want? Don't poll them; think like them. Remember, you are a reader first, writer second.

Week 5 :: Build a Manuscript

Foundation

Completion of Research

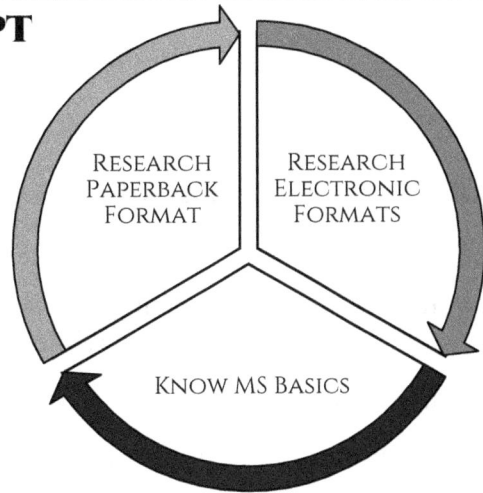

Research Paperback Format

Research Electronic Formats

Know MS Basics

Completion Chart

Day/ Date	Focus	Page Count	Word Count	Session Time
4	Front Matter			
5	Back Matter			
6				
7				
	Totals for this week			

Average this week's total word count with the total page count. …………………..

Transfer Total Words and Total Pages to the **Foundations** page, which precedes **Week 1**.

Increasing counts create a sense of accomplishment and reveal the power of persistence.

Calculating Words and Pages to Session Time helps determine if you are focused.

Reminder :: For those working with the e-book version, create your own template of the major charts or download them from www.writersinkservi.com website, under the Pro Writer Advice page.

5 :: 1 ~ RESEARCH PAPERBACK FORMAT

Formatting is the focus for this entire week.

Yes, your creative muse is taking a vacation. Use this time wisely. We need to work the analytical, editorial side of your brain while your creative muse takes a holiday.

Our focus is manuscript formatting. We need to know this before launching heavily into novel.

We wait until this point because you first need to discover if you have a story to work with. Once you know the Plot 7, you know if you have a story worth telling. Everything preceding merely set up those important scenes. Everything that comes after will build on them, increasing page and word count.

You don't want to be 250 pages into a manuscript—or finished—then have to return to every single paragraph to fix something.

Most print publishers who will create a paperback for you follow the Chicago Manual of Style. It has a few ticky differences from the styles you learned in high school and college (MLA and APA). Most of these ticky differences will not really matter in the long run although some of them (such as the serial or Harvard/Oxford comma) can throw certain readers out of the story.

For any ticky difference, whatever method you choose (such as not following the Harvard/Oxford comma or doing so) simply requires you to be consistent.

How do you know what's important? You don't, not the first few times around. So invest in a style manual and read it. Yes, I know it's boring.

Nowhere, however, will you read the current debate about spacing after a period (and semicolon and colon). Some people claim that you should only space once. Others swear by two spaces. Scientific studies (yes, I was shocked that scientists studied this, too) have discovered that the two spaces will assist with the readability of any text. Decide, and be consistent with that choice.

If you're writing in the hopes of contract with a traditional publisher or a smaller press, then they will have basic manuscript format rules under submission guidelines. These usually do not provide enough information for everything you need to know.

To set up your manuscript, pay particular attention to the following:

- Size of a paragraph indent (differs between print and electronic versions)
- Justification or left (or right) alignment only
- Page numbers—use and removal
- Special characters to denote breaks within chapters—and when those special characters will turn into gobbledygook in an uploaded manuscript.

- Styles—in word processing software, the Styles box sets up common font and spacing elements for chapter headings, main and sub- headings, and body text. Using Styles will help to create your own Table of Contents.
- Table of Contents creation
- Front Matter
- Back Matter
- Readers' Notes
- Acknowledgments

Always let the software program do its automatics: automatic text wrapping, for example, when you type to the end of a line and the machine automatically drops down to the next line.

For any formatting besides what was mentioned above, you should use the default settings on your word processing program. One-inch margins, 8 x 11 paper, etc.

Your job today is to find the manuscript formatting for print versions. Amazon's Kindle Publishing offers templates that explain paperback (ppb) formats and the changes necessary to align your manuscript with template requirements. This formatting is pretty universal (similar to Draft2Digital and Smashwords and Kobo, with a few changes). You can also investigate the formatting suggestions offered by Writers Digest magazine; this is standard formatting.

When you create a word document, you should save it as the *draft* or *paperback* version, which you can then alter for the e-book version. I start with the e-book version because I didn't consider paperback publication when I decided to publish my first book. I went with the largest e-book publisher and read their guidelines. Fortunately, it was not as difficult as I thought it would be.

Whenever I publish, I do run into the occasional difficulty, but the templates and the universal formatting solve most of the problems that I hear other writers complain about.

You should consider wide distribution. It's always on my list of things to do when I have more than twenty novels under one pseudonym. Not there yet, so I have not yet dipped a toe in the paperback distribution waters. It's coming, though, so I will have more research to do.

However, that research has nothing to do with formatting a manuscript, not really, and will be about the publishing process, not the writing process. Our focus is writing the novel.

Do the research and decide if you want to do a paperback or an e-book first.

Again, you need to do a clean manuscript, which will create fewer problems as you near the last page.

5 :: 2 ~ RESEARCH E-BOOK (OR ELECTRONIC) FORMAT

Remember to check the bulleted list in the previous section as you read through the templates and make notes for setting up your manuscript.

5 :: 3 ~ KNOW MS BASICS

Manuscript (MS) Basics is merely the proper way to use the software tools to ease your job.

Understanding your word processing software will enable you to get the best use from it.

Home Ribbon

Select a universal font like Times New Roman (no, it's not my first choice either) in size 12. Black color. You are selecting for an easily readable font. Choose a font that is standard worldwide, and you will have a better chance that it is acceptable. You will use *italics* for foreign words and phrases.

In the paragraph box, select Left Alignment and double spacing, removing the additional space between paragraphs. Use bullets for lists. On the back tab of Line and Page Breaks, check off the widow/orphan control as well as the keeps: "keep with next" and "keep lines together".

A handy little tool in the Paragraph box is the backwards paragraph symbol, ¶, which turns on visual formatting. Clicking it will show you spacing, tabbing, basically anything that you keyboard and nothing that is automatic.

Chapter headings are set up with styles. Right click as you hover over a Style type to modify the requirements: font, size, spacing, etc. Using Styles will keep everything uniform in the manuscript and will build your Table of Contents.

Insert a page break at the end of a chapter before starting the next one. Page breaks will maintain the separation.

Breaks within chapters, to denote a scene shift or a change in point of view, can be denoted with special characters. Don't get too crazy by using different fonts or unusual ones. Special glyphs are available, but many will turn into gobbledy-gook when uploaded. Stick with the special characters available in the Times New Roman font. Without going to special symbols, using the keyboard alone, you can create many different breaks with a variety of symbols. Be consistent within a manuscript.

A special area of the Home ribbon is Editing, which is usually helpful for finding and replacing words that you have realized were misspelled. However, selecting Find opens up a navigation window (or pane). Selecting *Headings* in the Navigation Pane gives you an outline of all your headings. When you search for a word or phrase and select *Results*, you see every area of your document where the search word occurs, enabling you to locate it quickly.

Layout

Under Margins, select one-inch top, bottom, left, right. This is standard. Orientation should be Portrait. Size only comes into play when changing the size for a paperback pdf version upload. When working with columns, you will need to understand section breaks. Read your software's Help information about section breaks.

References

The Table of Contents uses Styles. When you select the Automatic version (check to see how far the headings will result), the software program will build the TOC for you. This is a blessing. You can wait to build the TOC until the very end or you can build it early and update it throughout your writing.

If you have a nonfiction manuscript and want to use footnotes, you will find them under this area.

Review and View

Spellcheck, just like the thesaurus, can be deceptive. You think these processes are helpful; they actually are not. Software does not yet have the ability of fluid thinking, which is holding multiple rules in your head and dealing with the shifts between them.

If you select a certain location in your manuscript, you can have the software read it aloud for you.

You can track changes. I usually don't use this process, but I don't use a copy editor who marks up an electronic version. When judging between a print-out of the manuscript, most people find more errors in the print-out as opposed to reading solely on the computer screen.

If you use drawing objects, then go to View and Show. The ruler and gridlines are essential for placing objects and determining if they are within the proper margins.

Under Page Movement at View, you can select from Vertical (the way most software presents pages) or Side to Side. The latter is helpful when scanning for visual problems, such as drawn objects that are out of position.

More and File

At the left bottom of every screen page should be the page numbers, the location on the page, and the number of words. On the right bottom is the view and a quick zoom.

Under File, spend a little time reviewing the tabbed information under Options, which on my computer was hidden at the very bottom. You want to look at things that make your life easier. I have the habit of misspelling *the* as *hte* as well as other glitches with typing. I can set up Options to be helpful. Too much tinkering, however, only creates problems, so judge wisely.

Keyboard Short-cuts

- Ctrl + ' gives you an accent mark over your next typed letter: é. Other shortcuts for foreign language accent marks abound, or you can simply use the Insert > Symbol. Remember to stay in the font you are currently using.
- Ctrl + c will copy information that you have highlighted. With Ctrl you can put A for *select all*, V to paste what you have copied, B or U or I for bold or underline or italics, Z to undo a deletion, Y to redo something.
- ALT F7 brings up a synonym finder. Be wary of this. Not all synonyms have the exact meaning of the word you want to change.

You can find more keyboard shortcuts online. I prefer them to removing my hands from a keyboard to reach for the mouse.

5 :: 4 ~ FRONT MATTER

The Front Matter is the title page, boilerplate, table of contents, list of works, and any acknowledgements to people you want to thank.

The Title Page is for the title and the author (obvious) as well as the logo of your publishing company, if you have one (not so obvious).

A Boilerplate is the page in any print book on the reverse side of the title page. It contains the copyright notification, rights for this edition, publication notification (your explanation that this work is completely fictional rather than based on real people, a CYA), credit for the cover illustration and any interior illustrations, and brief contact information. You can model your standard rights and publication notification based on ones that you will see in other published books.

If you are selling your rights to a traditional publisher or a small press, then you will not include the Boilerplate.

You can place your List of Works before or after the table of contents. Acknowledgements come before the first chapters.

You can also have a Dramatis Personae, a list of characters with brief identifiers (also known as a Cast of Characters).

Create a standard document for your Front Matter and save it in a Publishing Folder in the File Explorer. You can adjust as needed and copy/paste for every manuscript after this one.

After this week's opening three days of research, you have finally generated words for this week.

5 :: 5 ~ BACK MATTER

Back Matter opens with your closing comments, such as Readers' Notes or glossaries or your Afterword or the *Raison d'Etre* for this work.

If you have End Notes, generated like Footnotes but placed together at the end, then they will come here.

Following the End Notes comes the promotional material. Promote your other books with brief descriptions or a teaser chapter. If you have no other books, then briefly mention the next novel with a title and a tagline (a teasing theme. See **1 :: 5**). Don't forget to provide your addresses or links to your website, email, and social media accounts.

Many indie writers (and the traditionally published are gradually converting) thank their readers then ask them to spread their enjoyment of the novel.

The Back Matter is also a standard document, updated for each successive book that you publish. Store it in your Publishing Folder in File Explorer.

Teaser chapters can be easily inserted into the Back Matter once you have it in your manuscript. Store them in the Publishing Folder as well. Title them appropriately so you can identify them at a glance. You may not return to this document for months. As you write more and more, however, and your speed kicks up, you will return to the Publishing Folder more often.

VISIONING

Record word and page counts, even when developing ideas rather than actually writing manuscript pages. These counts provide a sense of accomplishment.

Never delete the ideas that you develop. On Wednesday, you may decide to trash your writing; by Friday you may want those ideas back. Even if the ideas stay trashed, they may seed another book. Store any deleted work in an *ideas folder*.

WEEK	FOCUS	START DATE	END DATE	HOURS SPENT	WORD COUNT	PAGE COUNT
6	SEE YOUR PLOT					
7	SEE YOUR WORLD					
8	SEE YOUR PRIMARIES					
9	SEE YOURSELF WRITING					
10	SEE YOURSELF WRITING					

Total Number of Days Spent Writing :: ....

Total Word Count for Visioning :: ....

Average Number of Words per Day :: ....

Total Page Count for Visioning :: ....

Average Number of Pages per Day :: ....

Actual Page Count for Novel (not research) :: ....

Actual Word Count for Novel (not research) :: ....

As the story develops, these beginning ideas may change and even transform.

Story is organic and fluid; let it grow and flow.

FOR THOSE WORKING WITH THE E-BOOK VERSION, CREATE YOUR OWN TEMPLATE OF THE MAJOR CHARTS OR DOWNLOAD THEM FROM WWW.WRITERSINKSERVI.COM WEBSITE, UNDER THE PRO WRITER ADVICE PAGE

WEEK 6 :: ENVISION YOUR PLOT

COMPLETION CHART

DAY / DATE	FOCUS	PAGE COUNT	WORD COUNT	SESSION TIME
1	SEE THE 7 PLOT TYPES			
2	SEE THE TYPES TWIST			
3	SEE THE EFFECT ON THEME			
4	SEE THE ELEMENTS ~ A			
5	SEE THE ELEMENTS ~ B			
6				
7				
	TOTALS FOR THIS WEEK			

Average this week's total word count with the total page count. ....

Transfer Total Words and Total Pages to the **Visioning** page, which precedes this one.

Increasing counts create a sense of accomplishment and reveal the power of persistence.

Calculating Words and Pages to Session Time helps determine if you are focused.

6 :: 1 ~ SEE THE 7 PLOT TYPES

You will find arguments aplenty if you research the various plot types. Some say there's only the monomyth with endless variations. Some say there's only two: the Hero's Arc and the Heroine's Arc. Other say there are five or seven or ten or more.

Seven's a good number. In the language of symbols, it's the perfect number, so let's stick with seven.

In 2004, Christopher Booker published *The Seven Basic Plots: Why We Tell Stories*. (Yes, I know some people argue about him, but he does have literary insights.) He classified his seven using common language that everyone can understand.

I first discussed these seven basic plots in my book for newbie writers *Think like a Pro*, the first book in this series. I'm repeating some of that information here. You job this week is to discover which type of plot you think you are crafting into a book.

Here are the Seven Basic Plots, according to Booker. With his list, I have my own list of stories that fit each category, moving from concrete to abstract, literal to metaphorical, children's books to contemporary films and on to classic literature. My list of stories ranges from simplistic to literary. You should be able to fit your concept into one of the categories. That just starts your work.

Overcoming the Monster

Beowulf, Jaws, Lord of the Flies, King Lear, Alien, Pride and Prejudice, Fried Green Tomatoes, Atonement

- *Jaws* by Peter Benchley is an excellent example of a monster. The great white shark is pure animal, functioning from an animal's goals of survival and reproduction of itself. While it seems to have a vengeful drive, it actually only performs its animal goals of finding and killing and eating its prey. Very much like Herman Melville's *Moby Dick*, Jaws concerns itself with the characters hunting the creature. Melville does a much better job showing the revenge and greed that make monsters of men as well as presenting the few who can overcome these monsters.
- *Fried Green Tomatoes* by Fannie Flagg has several metaphorical monsters. SPOILERS if you haven't read the book or seen the movie. The first and strongest monster is the abusive husband who comes between Idgie and Ruth's uncommon love . The husband is killed by innocence. This monster's death is then made more monstrous because he is turned into barbecue and eaten by the sheriff who comes to investigate his disappearance. An additional monster is the railroad train that kills Idgie's brother and later takes the arm of Ruth's son (later called Stump). The cancer that kills Ruth is the third monster in the film.

Rags to Riches

Cinderella, Aladdin, Oliver Twist, Great Gatsby, Prince and the Pauper, Good Deeds, Pretty Woman

- Mark Twain's *The Prince and the Pauper* juxtaposes the lives of a prince and a poor boy by having them switch roles and encounter the trials that both face. The poor boy believes that a prince's life is easy and discovers that it is not, just as the prince discovers the freedom of the poor boy's life while his own is caged by the ceremony that surrounds a monarch.
- The film *Pretty Woman* follows an unusual call girl who falls for a billionaire. The call girl copes with the truth of her existence much better than the billionaire does, but she discovers her idea of love is ragged and torn. In being with the billionaire, her heart is mended. The billionaire realizes that, without love, he is poor and that his dreams of conquering the world through money only creates a poor-ness of self, of ethics and morals. Through the classic trope of a "call girl with a heart of gold", he sees the errors of his materialistic absorption—all without ever giving up his wealth.

The Quest

Watership Down, Raising Arizona, Willow, Raiders of the Lost Ark, Avatar, The Best Exotic Marigold Hotel, Northanger Abbey

- *Raiders of the Lost Ark* is a classic quest film, the archaeologist on the search for the greatest treasure of the ancient world. Indiana Jones searches for treasure in many different cultures. The greatest treasure of all, however, is love, which he finds when re-united with an old love (only to be re-separated after the film is over). The Nazis think they have the greatest treasure in the lost Ark of the Covenant. Opening the Ark of the Covenant destroys the Nazis in that location. The crated Ark winds up in a huge warehouse with other supposed-similar treasures. Quest found then lost again.
- Jane Austen's *Northanger Abbey* is about a young woman in search of adventure through entering high society and discovering a wealthy suitor. She is fascinated by racy novels of gothic mystery and looks for similar spooky mysteries around her, only to offend deeply the so-suitable suitor that she had found. She returns in disgrace to her family, wiser about the important things in life—and is rewarded when her treasured suitable suitor follows her to her home and proposes marriage.

Comedy

anything by Aristophanes, anything by the Marx Brothers, *Airplane, The Blues Brothers, Animal House, A Walk in the Woods, Arsenic and Old Lace, Bringing Up Baby, Much Ado about Nothing, A Midsummer Night's Dream, Mama Mia!*

- Shakespeare's *Much Ado About Nothing* is about crossed hearts, tricked hearts, and evil hearts that delight in causing problems. The humor comes from the quick repartee that cuts with its wit, the carnival dance with masks that conceal only to reveal, and the watchmen who don't see what is before them but still manage to resolve the problem that crossed the hearts. At the end, the two tricked hearts realize they are in love, after all.

- The classic Cary Grant / Katherine Hepburn comedy of *Bringing Up Baby* repeats the quick repartee of Shakespeare as well as crossed-up problems with a leopard and a spunky little dog, an aunt that can't hear and an uncle with ashes.

Tragedy

Oedipus, Macbeth, Rebel without a Cause, Frances, Philadelphia, Cool Hand Luke, Bonnie and Clyde, Whatever Happened to Baby Jane?

- The tragedy of *Cool Hand Luke* is the man who uses his wits only to subvert the establishment rather than improve himself. He seems to seek situations that will place in him direct conflict with law enforcement: when the film opens, he is cutting parking meters off their poles. His situation worsens as he challenges the prison guards, much like McMurphy in *One Flew Over the Cuckoo's Nest* challenges the medical guards in the psychiatric facility. Both men win the respect of their fellow inmates, but neither can win their battles against the established institutions.
- *Macbeth* presents a man whose ambition for the throne destroys his moral compass. He kills the king. He kills two innocent men and blames them for the king's murder. To hide what he's done, he kills his best friend. To keep control of the country he seizes, he kills many more people, although Shakespeare only shows us the deaths of a woman, her small child, and her baby. And the witches laugh with glee to bring a great man down.

Rebirth

Sleeping Beauty, Beauty and the Beast, A Christmas Carol, Now Voyager, Summertime, Avatar, Persuasion, Under the Tuscan Sun

- *Beauty and the Beast* has two rebirths. First, Beauty is reborn when she discovers that appearances matter not at all; the heart of a person is what matters. Appearances are actually deceptive; people's actions reveal their true selves. Second, Beast is reborn through Beauty's love. In the original story we are not told the reason that the Beast is cursed. His lonely trials through the years re-shape his personality and his character, transforming him from his former self worthy of the curse to a reborn person worthy of Beauty's love.
- *Now, Voyager* is a film that I avoided for years, having not understood the power of Bette Davis' films. I was wrong. Suffering under a domineering mother, Charlotte Vale emerges from her stifling cocoon. On a cruise which she takes to meet people who do not know the repressed girl that she had cast off, she discovers a man who loves her for herself. They cannot be together, even though he is unhappily married. In visiting the psychiatrist who helped her overcome her mother's domination, she connects with a young girl very much like her former self—only to discover that girl is the daughter of the man she loves. She resolves to help that girl achieve her own rebirth.

Voyage and Return

Peter Rabbit, The Hobbit, Odyssey, The Lion the Witch and the Wardrobe, Brideshead Revisited, Mansfield Park, Great Expectations, The Tempest

- The children's story *Peter Rabbit* seems simplistic on the surface. Out we go, get captured by the Farmer, escape but lose the coat off your back, and return home. On the way we discover that greed can get you in trouble, but through patience and persistence we can escape any cages placed around us. Family will always welcome us back, no matter what we have lost on our journey away.

- *Great Expectations* by Charles Dickens presents an orphan influenced by three abusive woman: a physically-abusive sister, an emotionally abusive rich woman, and a verbally abusive girl. All three warp his goals and motivations for life. He ignores the lessons of the gentle blacksmith and the good-hearted young woman who can teach him how to read what is important in life just as she taught him how to read books. A chance encounter offers him great fortune, but he wastes it trying to become someone worthy of the verbally abusive girl. He loses the girl, he loses the money, he loses what's best in life, all because he put his expectations on the wrong things.

Writing Goal ~ Select Your Plot Type

You should be able to fit your concept into one of the categories. That just starts your work. Using my summaries of a guide, write a quick summary of your story based on that category. Keep tying your story elements to your plot type, working with the literal and metaphorical meanings of the category.

6 :: 2 ~ SEE THE PLOT TYPES TWIST

I know you are desperate to get to your work, and you can skip today if you just can't wait any longer.

Being forced to wait is sometimes helpful. Sometimes, though, it kills creativity. After a break, we stumble when we try to start running. You can move ahead if you desire.

I would, however, come back to this exercise at a later date. This exercise will stretch your ability to see story as a writer, rather than a reader or a viewer. It builds the necessary skills of analysis and synthesis.

Analysis is the breaking into many parts; synthesis is putting those parts into a new form. Writers use these two higher critical thinking skills constantly. We constantly take a character in a particular situation and break down the parts of the story before reforming all of those parts into a coherent new story.

Writing Goal ~ Twist Your Knowledge of Stories into the Categories

For each of the seven categories, write your own summary of a book or film that fits the heading. Try to build a good summary as I did with *Fried Green Tomatoes* and *Great Expectations*. You are looking for the key elements of the story that fit the category.

You may select from my list or work with your chosen book / film or look for a blogger who has created a list for each category.

As you work with the summaries, you may see connections in your own concept, such as the three kinds of abuse (*Great Expectations*) or metaphors that you could play with (*Now Voyager*'s cocoon and butterfly) or contrasts (*Beauty and the Beast* or *Pretty Woman)* or even similarities with other works (*Cool Hand Luke* to *One Flew over the Cuckoo's Nest*) that you didn't see before.

6 :: 3 ~ SEE THE PLOT TYPE'S EFFECT ON THEME

Previously, you spent an entire writing session on theme at **1 :: 5**. Maybe the theme came easily, and you drifted off to do other things. Maybe you gave up and abandoned the tagline.

If you blew off the assignment at **1 :: 5**, you need to fix it now.

This look at theme is focused on your chosen Plot Type. Do they connect? If they do not, then nudge a few words to see the connection.

The theme or tagline will serve as the guide for your promotional copy, the blurb that will be on the back cover or in the electronic store. It may be the only thing that will fit in the limited 25-word ad that you run after publication. It will be the only thing that can fit in the limited space you have on certain promotional materials.

Every element of your story ties to your theme, whether it guides the selection of your scenes or your character's actions and reactions or your metaphors and symbols in your descriptions and exposition.

Stories will always have multiple themes. The tagline theme is for the central plot and your protagonist's main focus.

Writing Goal ~ See your Final Theme

Does this theme connect to your selected category? While you should not use the category words in your theme sentence, the connection should be obvious.

Can you brainstorm a list of 33 words that connect your tagline theme to your category?

- Yes, this exercise can be helpful. Write this list without judging any word's worth. If you start with *battle* and head into kisses, follow where the intuitive muse leads.
- By the way, that number 33 didn't just come out of my whoopsie-daisy. For many years I worked with writing-resistant students.. Through repetition of this exercise, both my students and I discovered that the first words will start your mind thinking but are never the significant ones. The significant words come after passing #10 or #15.
- Students who were word-facile (large vocabularies) didn't reach the significant words until they were nearly finished, and the best writers often had to go beyond 33. Keep going until the flood of words stops—or your hand protests. I wouldn't go past # 50; that's just throwing words onto the page.
- You will hit static a little before or after #15. Static means that your brain will rebel and refuse to offer any words. Sometimes, you can break the static by just writing down any words. Sometimes, you turned on the critical editor and rejected a word that your creative muse offered you. When you hit static, back up several words and start writing again. Never erase, just shift over and continue.

Does your working title for the manuscript connect to your tagline theme? That connection can be literal or metaphorical.

Keep your tagline theme to a single sentence. Can you twist the sentence around so that it is in active form (not passive) and has no more than 12 words?

If you complete all of these suggestions, you should now have an excellent tagline theme.

6 :: 4 & 6 :: 5~ See the Elements A & B

This exercise asks you to view your story through its category based on three elements.

Each of the seven basic plots has three elements that make the category individual rather than uniform. Explanations for each element follow these directions.

Viewing any story from other standpoints can be illuminating.

Consider *Atonement*, an Overcoming the Monster plot. When you consider it as a Rags to Riches, the male hero's story gains a power distinct from the younger sister's monstrous character arc.[2]

Writing Goals ~ Looking through New Eyes

For today, find your category and work through the three elements.

For tomorrow, read through the other categories. Tilt your head a little sideways by thinking outside of the category box. Do any of the questions for the three elements in the other categories give you ideas? That's the purpose.

If you blow off this exercise now, then remember to come back later if you hit an obstacle and write yourself into a corner. Opening your perspective on the story can give insights that help you work out of corners.

Also for tomorrow, consider running parallel story arcs, the primary plot category for your protagonist(s) and a secondary and different plot category for your antagonist. Different plot arcs for your central primaries will deepen your writing.

A mirrored plot, reversing the images of protagonist and antagonist, is another plotting technique.

Overcoming the Monster

This category is not as simple as it seems. We often have difficulty overcoming monsters in our lives. Our daily monsters are not as easily identified as they are in films and classic genre books. The daily monster can be a scaring and scarring evil with blood-stained claws. Be it a vampire or merely a life-sucking job, a philandering spouse or an oppressive dictator, all are monsters who destroy other lives.

The invidious monsters are the ones who seem friendly, the ones who seem to help our protagonist, the ones who would never, not in a million years, do anything to hurt anyone.

(1) To write deeper than any basic genre, have your protagonist struggle to identify the real monster.

---

[2] All of the three elements from the Seven Basic Plots are an abbreviated excerpt from *Think like a Pro*.

(2) We have to acquire the tools needed to defeat the monster. Buffy the Vampire Slayer had a rigorous training schedule; our protagonist must train as well. If that monster is a life-sucking boss, how can the protagonist re-set the boundaries between job and life? How will the philandering spouse be discovered? What will enlighten the protagonist to the invidious monsters who present themselves as friends? How will the now-aware protagonist develop the skills necessary to step up and stand against the seemingly-innocent monster?

(3) The actual battle often requires the sacrifice of something dear, with no guarantee that anything will ever replace our sacrifice.

Rags to Riches

In badly-written rags-to-riches stories, logic is tossed out as writers drag their protagonists into the luxurious wealth that they think their character deserves. In well-written stories, the protagonist is shown developing the skills necessary to gain wealth and succeed in that new environment.

Logic tells us that no one receives something (great) for nothing.[3] The impoverished state needs to be presented along with the dream of greatness that the protagonist has. That dream should be possible, not improbable. **(1)**

The steps from rags to riches are presented. **(2)** What will each step entail? Who/what is essential to gaining the skills that are part of each step? Who/what will block the step?

The wealth needs to be reasonable. **(3)** Not everyone is descended from royalty or nobility, you know. Some of us were dirt farmers eager to escape our serfdom. (Welcome to America!) Not everyone will walk into a top editor position just because of an association with a mysterious billionaire.

By the way, what is wealth? Money? Time? Or knowledge? Or relationships? If no money is ever obtained but relationships are deepened, isn't that an example of the best riches in the world? (Preaching. Sorry. Not.)

The Quest

Searching for a treasure (tangible or intangible) requires a long journey to distant places in order to achieve a goal—whether that is a physical journey encountering exotic people for material treasure or an intellectual journey encountering exotic ideas for spiritual treasure. Thus, the three elements require ~

Remove the protagonist from the settled, day-to-day existence as the first required step. **(1)** The writer must present that mundane existence, showing the protagonist's contrasting satisfaction and dissatisfaction. An impelling event must drive the protagonist into the quest. What is the protagonist's quest? What makes the treasure so necessary to be obtained? The protagonist will be uncomfortable and awkward as s/he launches into the quest; however, the dissatisfaction is strong enough that remaining in the status quo is not an option.

Exhibit the entrance to the place completely new. **(2)** Know your story's definition of exotic. How is this new place exotic / different from what the protagonist has known before? How are the people in this new place also part of the exotic experience for the protagonist? What is charming

---

[3] If you think that, I have a bridge in Brooklyn that I'd like to sell you.

about the exotic experience? What remains unsatisfactory, preventing the new place from becoming a paradise?

Discovery of the treasure is like an epiphany. **(3)** Whether it's the pot at the end of the rainbow that the protagonist finds and uses to improve life back home or the discovery of something richer than was ever anticipated, how is that treasure discovered? Is it at first mistakenly avoided or ignored? If so, what brings the protagonist's attention back to it? How is the treasure a great richness? Does the treasure create such a temptation that return to the ordinary world is no longer a requirement?

Comedy

In writing story, we distinguish between humor and comedy.[4] Humor is telling jokes. Comedy is the protagonist achieving his goal. I fought the mis-definition of comedy in my classroom. It seems simple enough to write comedy. However, I will note that in comedy, pathos (deeply emotional moments) occur quite a good bit (while tragedies are often filled with humor).

The protagonist confronts adversity. **(1)**

That adversity is deepened through a series of confusing events. **(2)**

The climax clears up all confusion and grants the protagonist the original goal which has transformed in an unexpected way. **(3)**

To understand more about comedy, look at the information on tragedies and go in the opposite direction. Comedy is the expectation of tragedy, elevated emotionally through the escape of dire events.

Tragedy

In Comedy, all is achieved; in tragedy, all is futile. While death is not a requirement of tragedy, doom is. Writers of tragedy, to prevent unrelenting darkness, will often fill a tragedy with humor. Shakespeare is a master of keeping the audience engaged in the tragic form: *Romeo and Juliet* and *Macbeth* have several laugh-out loud moments that relieve the ratcheting suspense.

The protagonist—through his own actions—causes his own destruction. **(1)** An inner flaw (consider one of the Seven Deadly Sins[5] when constructing a story) sets in motion a domino effect.

While all may seem confused to the protagonist, we can see the steps that bring him to doom. At some point, usually toward the plot's center, the protagonist takes an irrevocable step. **(2)**

The protagonist may see the doom's approach. If he doesn't believe it, he continues forward without check. Most protagonists will act to reverse the approaching doom. How the protagonist confronts his doom is equally key: will he run away, or will he lean into it? **(3)**

Rebirth

---

[4] Hollywood doesn't, but Hollywood's not about story; it's about making money using the lowest common denominator possible [usually ridicule, usually raunchiness, usually violence, always sex]. Hollywood says that comedy is a show with lots of laugh. Nope. Just nope.

[5] 7 Deadly Sins: pride, wrath, greed, gluttony, sloth, lust, envy

Transformation occurs through reformation.

A special branch of the Rebirth story is apotheosis, when the protagonist is transformed into a god.

While *Eat, Pray, Love* is often given as an excellent example of a Rebirth plot, I think better examples are *Wild* and *Under the Tuscan Sun*. *Wild* contains a physical and intellectual transformation. *Under the Tuscan Sun* is a three-part reformation of self: the protagonist is no longer intellectually or physically or spiritually the person she was at the beginning.

A mirror is needed. Some starkly clear representation occurs that awakens the protagonist to "a better life". **(1)**

The protagonist launches into an attempt to achieve that better life, with flashes of insight and stumbling steps, all of which teach the protagonist how to change from who s/he is into who s/he wants to become. **(2)**

Eventually, a new self emerges, often in a new place. **(3)**

Voyage and Return

This plot category seems very similar to the Quest, except the goal is the return back to the original existence, wiser through the experienced trials and ordeals of the journey.

Normal existence for the protagonist must be presented as exactly what is wanted. **(1)** The reason for the journey should be dire: destruction of that existence is threatened. (*Identity Thief*'s character portrayed by Jason Bateman is the perfect example.)

The voyage itself may not be "exotic"; it may even seem ordinary on the surface, but it is enriching. **(2)** It may simply be getting back home, older but not necessarily wiser. Many different kinds of events will occur on this voyage. Great internal transformation will not occur. The goal of this voyage is not a treasure; the goal may not even be specified. If it is specified, then the goal will have much to do with returning home.

Returning home may have obstacles, as events and people may have conspired to work against the protagonist's easy settling back into the life that s/he loves. **(3)** Thus, the return may be the point of greatest difficulty for the protagonist. However, when all problems are overcome, the life that was threatened is restored, and the sun shines once again on the protagonist and what s/he holds most dear.

WEEK 7 :: ENVISION YOUR WORLD

COMPLETION CHART

DAY/ DATE	FOCUS	PAGE COUNT	WORD COUNT	SESSION TIME
1	SEE THE BASIC WORLD			
2	SEE THE STOMPING GROUNDS			
3	SEE THE BACKSTORY			
4	WORLD BUILDING A			
5	WORLD BUILDING B			
6				
7				
	TOTALS FOR THIS WEEK			

Average this week's total word count with the total page count. …………………..

Transfer Total Words and Total Pages to the **Visioning** page, which precedes Week 6.

Increasing counts create a sense of accomplishment and reveal the power of persistence.

Calculating Words and Pages to Session Time helps determine if you are focused.

7 :: 1 ~ SEE THE BASIC WORLD

This week we will build the world of your novel.

As with any of these early sections, if you want to skip right on past them and start writing, you may. They will sit here waiting on you, when you run into a stoppage. You will. Having background information prevents a lot of the barriers that interrupt white-hot creative flow.

By the way, don't call any stoppage **Writer's Block**. It usually means that the novel is missing something. Or it could be assorted fears (that's what drives most procrastination) or inertia and stagnation (which won't happen if you keep moving forward).

You may not have a lot of countable words this week, but you will definitely have work that will show your novel advancing.

Fictional Locations vs. Real Locations

Yes, it's perfectly fine for a writer of fiction to use real places. Yet even novels that have "real" locations add in fictional places to suit the author's needs for locations.

Every book in Paris will have a mention of the Eiffel Tower, the burnt Notre Dame Cathedral, the Louvre, or *Rive Gauche*. The people in those locations and the events happening to them will be fictional.

The Paris café where your protagonist meets her friends for crepes and coffee before heading off to sketch tourists should come wholly out of your imagination. You might base that café on one that you have seen and even where you had crepes and coffee for your own *petite dejeuner*, but your imagination can give the place a new name, a new waiter, and a new street where it can lead to the Seine.

You might base your novel on events that really happened. Your take on the people and those events will be fictional.

While real people in these places dealing with these events might fascinate you, any professional writer will advise you to go with fiction, not reality. To write about actual people of the past 150 years is to open your arms and embrace lawsuits. This is a sad commentary on reality. Someone's life might fascinate you, but their family may not be fascinated by what you write.

You can always have famous and infamous people walk through your stories. Their entry provides verisimilitude. Adding them is not wholly necessary, though, and they do not have to take an active part.

See It.

Already, you have in mind various areas where you want events to occur. You may have vivid visions of those places. You could have possibly taken photographs or found images online, either through browsing or looking for specific places in stock photo retailers like Shutterstock or Deposit Photos and the like.

Or you may simply have a general description: local bar filled with smoke, the willow pond with its overflow dam, the glass-encased office building with its high-speed elevators. You may think you are specific if you think "frontier America before the Revolutionary World" or Bond Street in London during the Regency era or the battle of Hastings in 1066.

These are *places* and *times*. Setting is more than place and time. It's also culture.

Think about your high school days. How many cultures can you name? The drama geeks, the band nerds, the hoodies, the jocks—of which the football guys had a different culture from the basketballers who were different from the cross-country runners. And we haven't even touched the teachers, who have their own various cultures not dependent upon their faculty domain and who should *never* be confused with the administration or the support personnel, who are often more vital than administration in the running of the school.

In each culture, the common behavior, focus, and personalities are greatly different.

So when you think *setting*, for each area, you should think about the different cultures who congregate in those places, often at different times.

In any modern bar, we have different cultures entering, each giving the setting a different vibe.

- People come in just after work then leave after an hour or two, either to get something to eat or to stop procrastinating about going home to their non-loved ones.
- We have the people who come in after dinner and linger all evening, for various reasons.
- Some people start drinking at Happy Hour and continue until closing.
- The bartender's personality will be vastly different depending on the time or fellow workers.
- The grunt is the bartender in training fetches the kegs or slices the lemons and limes or brings in ice.
- We have the waiters, competing for tips, undermining the new ones, ragging on the regular customers, flirting with the new guys.

Re-consider the *places* you have found for your story. Re-consider the *times* your characters will be there. Don't just think about what will *happen in your novel* when you look at setting. Think about what happens before your novel events occur. Consider this world in its *normal* situation before you introduce your conflict.

Once you've considered the normal reality for the places you already have imagined, do a little search on stock photo retailers. These images will help you describe the places for your potential audience.

Descriptive elements ground the audience into the story. Having images in hand when you start the rough draft prevents you from breaking the writing flow. Print them off. Label them. Stick the images where you will see them as you write.

Job 1

With the settings you have located for your stories, determine what the environment is like when things are *normal*.

Job 2

Locate images to use when writing descriptions by browsing stock photo retailers.

Job 3

Create captions as labels with descriptive elements noted either as part of the captions or on the back of the images.

7 :: 2 ~ STOMPING GROUNDS

Now it's time to discover the basic locations for each of your primary characters.

Job 1

Know your primary characters' stomping grounds.

A stomping ground is the local neighborhood. Friends, family, local hang-outs, local shops and restaurants and groceries, people who serve as authority and people who rebel against that authority: all of these are essentials for any stomping ground, and your characters interact with these people.

Job 2

Consider religious, medical, educational, entertainment, and fitness locations.

Add in the services that people need on a constant basis, such as gasoline stations. Take a drive around your own stomping grounds. Really see what's on each street and major side street.

Map the Stomping Grounds

Draw a map of your primary characters' stomping grounds. You should do this for both the protagonist and antagonist if the events of your novel place them in constant interaction.

If areas in a house or a workplace are important to your primaries, draw the building plan. If you know that a building complex or a multi-story building will provide several locations for scenes, draw that.

How detailed should you be? Generally, entrances and exits (including elevators), light sources, and basic layouts distinguishing public from private access are helpful.

Closer details such as closets where people probably shouldn't hide, cubicles where people can get lost in the rat maze, and side caves where monsters lurk will depend upon the requirements of your novel.

Having these basic layouts of areas and buildings will save you so much time later on. Until the moment you publish, these layouts are considered *draft* form. You can change at will. Once you publish, save the layouts but don't alter them. You can make additions—which is the primary reason *not* to become too detailed.

7 :: 3 ~ SEE THE BACKSTORY

Backstory is one of those detailed information dumps that you the writer will need to have but that readers will likely never see.

Info dump is exactly what it says: You have information that you shove into a story when it serves no plot purpose or character revelatory purpose.

It's a *dump* because readers will plow through and think, "This is all junk that should have been thrown out." Worse, readers might start skimming to get past the info dump and miss a vital element when the story starts back. Then, when they get to the end, they believe the writer didn't put that vital element in—and diss you because it was missing, which it wasn't.

You don't want to spend a lot of time on backstory. It's necessary but not essential to story.

Map People.

Mapping people means that you are creating the backstories for your primaries and secondaries. Backstories create motivation and automatic behavior reactions of people. Flinching at loud noises can have multiple causes: the backstory will tell you the reason that it occurs.

You might write 150 to 200 words then use only a snippet. To add 140 useless words to your story will become info dump, which we want to avoid. Never consider that backstory is useless. It adds depth and richness. It just doesn't go in your novel.

Places also have backstory. The *history* of a particular place is not how it came to be. That history will provide what happened to *people* in that place. Whether a tragic event occurred or the place's founding was important, you should consider a quick brief for each significant place. Remember, this brief will focus on people in that place.

These backstories will be a mine of information as you are writing. They help provide opinions and automatic reactions of characters to other people's actions and reactions as well as events and situations.

Refer back to your work on your main characters as you consider backstory. You may already have sketched out this information.

Secondary characters are those who interact with the primaries throughout the story. Their backstories will be very brief.

If you have in mind a tertiary character with a strong motivation for betrayal or alliance, you may wish to add in their backstory. A character who provides only a snippet of vital information may also have a backstory which you should briefly--50 words or so--note.

7 :: 4 ~ WORLD BUILDING A

World-Building is what we've been doing. Whole books have been written about this subject. The speculative fiction genres of fantasy and science fiction require it, and several writers have published their own books, including detailed information about drawing your own world.

If you work in the speculative fiction genres, then invest in these long-term references. If you cannot afford the investment, then add them to your Wish List as a high priority for others to buy for you.

The Reasons for World Building

People function together through a variety of systems, whether hierarchical/political or natural.

In a contemporary mystery, when you throw your protagonist into jail (*gaol*, in British English), you need to know the jargon of the law enforcement system. A character who receives probation is vastly different from one who gets out on parole. Whatever world you plan to create as the dominant *culture* of your novel, know the particular jargon that fits that world.

In life, we have whole sets of field-related jargon that we truly don't understand. Whenever you use a word that is specific to a field, do ensure that you know the specific meaning.

When you create the world of your novel, you also need to ensure that you understand how that world works.

Nothing will jar readers out of a novel faster than your mis-use of a word that they use daily. Even contemporary novels must know their worlds.

Here is my own partial list that I usually work through when creating my own world. Sometimes I work through every item on the list; usually, I don't. However, as of this writing, I'm over 20 books into fiction writing (counting all my pseudonyms), with a growing number of non-fiction books.

When I began writing fantasy—you know, in the Dark Ages—I filled a three-inch ring binder with such diverse topics as weapons, food, sample names, locations, rank and status, and my own card game. This was a thick **Master Book of the Book**. I broke away from that world for over a decade before I picked it back up when I began publishing. The binder was extremely helpful to remind myself of the world as I revised that earlier, juvenile novel.

Most world-building occurs when you want to create a world completely separate from your own. If you are writing of a different culture in a different part of our real world, you will need to build that world so you are not constantly researching the language, the social and governmental hierarchies, the plants and animals, the food and eating habits, the religion and its traditions and holidays, and a host of other things that we take for granted.

How do you start world-building?

We start with the Stomping Ground. From there, you consider how the Stomping Ground fits into the world at large.

Basic terms can trip you up, so never assume. For example, a city has a cathedral along with churches while a town only has churches. A village has a church while a hamlet does not. The distinction comes from what the population can support, not from the size of the population alone.

Libraries and museums and theatre usually require a population with a higher level of education. All communities have methods by which they entertain themselves, whether it's vendors such as cinemas or organized recreation such as softball leagues.

Whether historical or contemporary, real or speculative, you can build your world simply by considering your own world. Your current and past life serves as a model for your novel.

Stories are never in a vacuum. Even the space stations of science fiction have locations analogous to our contemporary world. A short list include the ship berths at docks, warehousing, shops and workplaces, central government and business enterprises, entertainment and meeting spaces, services and commerce (think repair shops and banks), agricultural areas, educational services, and cultural areas.

While you do not have to delve into all of the following as well as tomorrow's work, you should have a good understanding of how these will occur.

Often, in building the world, you discover intriguing snippets to add to your story, like J.K. Rowling's horrible candies of atrocious names and her development of the game quidditch, which becomes a necessary plot element in every book. These intriguing snippets will set your work apart from other similar stories and provide opportunities for licensing the snippets to game, toy, and clothing businesses as well as many more opportunities.

Basic Considerations

- **Communication**: how does it occur within the stomping grounds and beyond to the region: local, state, national, and international. What areas would have better technology? Why?
- **Medical** establishments are necessary for treating diseases and wounds. Basic hygiene prevents the spread of diseases. The level of medical care is dependent upon the level of communication and technology as well as the support received from an enlightened ruling authority.
- **Civil authority**, elected or appointed or inherited, that controls from region to world. How does the civil authority maintain its power? Through **law enforcement,** which always begins local. The enforcers of the law are not the makers of the law nor are they the punishers of the law. Consider the **legislative** and **justice** systems. In your world, are these three separate entities? Modern first world societies have separated these institutions; however, in antiquity, these institutions are closely connected.
- Law enforcement is considered separate from the **military** (an armed force controlled by the government for the sole purpose of the defense of the nation from encroaching nations). The military is land and sea and air (based on the level of technology).
- While education has developed modern distinctions based on age, the learning remains based on the principals of **grammar**, **preparatory**, and **scholarship**. Grammar Schools provide rudimentary learning that the majority will receive. Complex preparatory learning leads to

greater scholarship. Professional learning requires intense scholarship to master.

- Socio-economic demographics create a modern **caste system**. In the past, birth (the blue-bloods) inherited their ruling status. In the United States, we glorify people of great wealth or celebrity that has given them great wealth, whether they deserve their glorification or not. We mistake infamy for fame. What will be the strata of your society?

- Religion has had a strong role in developing our daily lives. Our weekly, monthly, and yearly **calendars** are based on religious observances. Holidays were formerly the only special observances of the year.

- What will be your **pantheon** of gods? (Yes, even in your contemporary novels, the characters will have gods, whether they are the gods of the major religions of our world or scientific beliefs.) The ancient Greeks, while worshipping their gods, also ridiculed virtually every one of their deities. Other cultures feared their gods and would not dare be **sacrilegious**. The ancient Greeks also believed their gods were immortal, yet Norse gods knew they would die. All the ancient religions practiced human sacrifice, from the ancient druids to the Aztecs and even the Greeks. For example, an earlier *chronological* event in the *Iliad* is Agamemnon's sacrifice of his daughter Iphigenia so the ships can launch for Troy. That human sacrifice exhibited his depravity as well as shows the modern reader that Homer's appalled listeners had abandoned the practice of their past.

- **Religions** also can be government-approved or not, accepted by the government but considered mere superstition by the social elite, or an outright rebellion against the government. In any society, more than one denomination of a single religion will occur; people cannot agree on doctrinal rules. Cities will have not just an abundance of denominations but also of different religions. Some of those religions will be accepted, several will be on the fringes of acceptability, and a few will be underground. Some religions accept that the 7 Deadly Sins remain sinful; some allow two or three of those sins under certain conditions.

- Just as a society can have many views of religion, that same society will have many divergent morés related to **intimacy** and sexual encounters. Intimacy builds relationships. How will relationships between intimates be formalized? Will relationships be imposed upon people who are not intimates (as marriages of the upper classes in medieval times were contractual, for the gain of status, lands or wealth rather than based on the growth of a relationship)? What will be the basic **family structures** in your world?

- **Technology** affects not only communication and the military but also a country's infrastructure. What will the technology allow? What cannot occur because of the technology or restrictions by authorities on the use of technology? Will you have underground technology?

As you develop these areas, whether you go into great detail or you just make a couple of notes, you should watch for anachronisms or anatopisms.

7 :: 5 ~ WORLD BUILDING B

Yesterday, the World Building dealt with socio-political systems, artificial constraints on people. Today, we look at the **natural constraints** on people.

You may have thought World Building was only topographical.

And it is. Have you considered your world's ~?

- Mountains and valleys, plains and swamps.
- Forests, meadows, pastures, and fields (tilled acreage).
- Ponds, lakes, oceans and streams, creeks, rivers—waterfalls and cascades. Dams and river locks.
- Frontiers and borders. How will the borders be maintained?
- Old ruins and traces of previous civilizations almost lost to time.

Understand the regions and the **climates** of those regions. How will weather systems work? How will people cope with the extremes of the weather?

Two things greatly affected by climate are food and clothing.

- **Food** sources: farms, packagers, local markets and brick-and-mortar stores. Seasonal goods and specialty items.
- **Clothing** sources: how does the clothing get to the purchaser? Who makes each item of clothing, from woven cloth to leather? Clothing is chosen by climate and season. Personal **ornamentation**, from jewelry to tattoos, is considered clothing. Such personal items not only have sentimental attachment but can also be worn to show groups to which a person belongs.

A society's level of civilization affects the **four basics of life**: sunlight, clean water, clean air, and good soil. First-world civilizations struggle with pollution of water and soil and smog that affects air and sunlight. Third-world countries struggle to find good water and soil and may have sources that are polluted through inadequate hygiene.

- How will the people of your novel have access to these four?
- Will they be so common that they're taken for granted? Or will they require filters for use?
- Will finding water be drudgery, as it was on farms before wells were dug and buckets had to be carried from local creeks and ponds?
- Will people jog along smog-filled streets? Will every step outside be an encounter with bad air?

Large cities provide green spaces for their citizens. Small towns have easy access to the natural world. How do the green spaces change when the weather changes? How does access change?

While the presence of something means that we take it for granted, the **Absence** can be as remarkable.

- On a space station, how the local institutions might provide representations of nature and the reasons for those representations can provide intriguing asides for your primary characters.
- Consider the access that people will have to certain locations. I read widely. Of late, in several books set on space stations, I have encountered ordinary characters who retreat to agricultural pods in order to connect to nature or to have a bit of privacy. While they're enjoying the green spaces, I'm wondering why the authorities aren't worried about contamination of food and water sources.
    - What allows ordinary people to have access into such privileged areas?
    - Even more interesting, how did other people who are not allowed into the agricultural pod function without connection to the green world?

Transportation across the natural world from one location (a farm) to another (a city) is affected by infrastructure which is dependent on technology. When working beyond our contemporary world, consider how transportation occurs. Consider the difficulties of road building, traveling those roads, and the time that travel would take using the common methods of travel.

- In science fiction, space travel follows laws. While you do not need to know (or convey to the reader) the nuts and bolts of your FTL engine, you need to create rules for your *faster than light* travel. If you use wormholes, do you need FTL? Listening to film buffs criticize a film for breaking its own rules about hyperjump helps us realize the importance of following rules that we have set up.
- The colonial frontier stopped at the Appalachian Mountains until Daniel Boone found the Cumberland Gap. Fifteen miles became a common distance between towns because of how long it took to travel between them and back to the homestead. Historical novelists should consider not just how long it takes to travel a distance but the difficulties of travel as well as the reason for the difficulties.
- Time Travel will also operate by particular laws, and several speculative fiction works have pondered the problems when travelers change a historic event.

Magic, while supernatural, is considered *natural*. It functions by many of the same laws that govern the physical world.

- How do the laws of your magic operate? I advise you not to make your magic users omnipotent, like a god. If a user of magic is unstoppable, how can s/he be stopped when s/he becomes a threat to society?
- Is your magic grounded in the elements? Does it function like lightning?
- What affect does the use of magic have on its user? How is magic acquired? How does someone train to use magic?
- What can oppose this magic? What are the rules of the opposing power?
- Who cannot use magic? What determines who can wield magic and who cannot?
- Since magical users can go "rogue", how can they be punished? What will "cage" their magic?

Lastly, if at all possible, create an Image Board of key locations and maps and house/space station plans and other specific elements. You can purchase a large foam board or a science tri-fold project board. If you get tired of visitors seeing your world and yapping about your writing, a tri-fold project board can be stowed in your closet whenever they come. ☺

WEEK 8 :: ENVISION YOUR SECONDARIES & MORE

COMPLETION CHART

DAY/ DATE	FOCUS	PAGE COUNT	WORD COUNT	SESSION TIME
1	BFFs OR NOT			
2	FOILS AND OBSTACLES			
3	2 ADDITIONAL SIDE CHARACTERS			
4	WALK-ONS & CAMEOS			
5	MINIONS OF EVIL			
	TOTALS FOR THIS WEEK			

Average this week's total word count with the total page count. ....

Transfer Total Words and Total Pages to the **Visioning** page, which precedes Week 6.

Increasing counts create a sense of accomplishment and reveal the power of persistence.

Calculating Words and Pages to Session Time helps determine if you are focused.

A FEW WORDS ON WEEK 8

Secondary and Tertiary characters often capture the reader's attention. Great secondary characters—Team members—who support the protagonist can easily turn into primary characters for a sequel, one after another until you have a whole series set in your built world. Who wouldn't want to read a book about Legolas from *The Lord of the Rings* trilogy? Many romance writers create a family then subsequently marry off the brothers and sisters to their heart's desires in later books.

Build your secondary characters in the same manner as your primaries. You do not have to work in such close details, but the basic elements should be covered. Even if you do not currently have ideas for a sequel or a series, you have created depth for your novel. Your subconscious will also start swirling these characters around in your head. Before you know it, another situation pops out.

For each of the secondaries, develop the following basic information:

1. Goal
2. Motivation
3. Conflict
4. Dear Desire
5. Stressor
6. Nadir
7. Zenith

8 : 1 ~ BFFS OR NOT

A BFF (just in case you didn't know) is a Best Friend Forever. This character is the protagonist's deepest friend.

Although most best friends are formed in the childhood or teen-aged years (or even college), time is not the determining factor for the best friend. Common interests draw people together. Common ideas about the world cement a friendship. Common goals for the future are not necessary.

No matter what, a BFF will face oncoming fire, shoulder to shoulder, the ultimate ally. Shared sadness and tragedies create iron-strong links that only the decaying rust of emotional pain can begin to destroy. Years may pass, distance may intervene, but true friends will rally around when they are needed.

If we were discussing **Team Roles** from the professional world, the ally character would be classified as the Follower or Fulfiller [Role 2] of the protagonist leader's goal. Additional team roles (besides the leader [Role 1]) are the Advocate / Questioner [Role 3] and the Unifier / Resolver [Role 4], both of equal importance as allies but required to be BFFs.

Strong allies can be as honorable and worthy as the protagonist, but most will have a weakness than can be exploited at the worst times. These weaknesses explain the reason that they are not the leaders of the team.

Writing Goal for the Ally

In addition to the 7 areas (e.g., goal, stressor, zenith), answer the following?

- Describe this character. (If you're working with a team, do this section for each member.)
- How did the ally meet the protagonist?
- What commonality ties them together?
- How did s/he become an ally?
- Will the status of ally remain to the end of the book, or will that status be destroyed? (Read on about the SAlly before you answer this question.)
- Will your antagonist have an ally? Why or why not?

A special form of this character is the Confidante.

The confidante has specific duties beyond that of BFF or ally. This character knows the protagonist's secrets (not the heart secrets, but all of the others). When the protagonist becomes mired in despair, the confidante knows what to say to drive her/him out of that mucky mess.

It is often the death of the confidante that hurts readers so much. They might anticipate the death of another character, but surely the writer won't kill the confidante? Surely the writer will kill a character with flaws, especially those flaws that create a weakness in the protagonist? Surely we *will* kill that confidante if the story demands it. The confidante's death becomes especially hard to bear when s/he has survived earlier lethal situations, perhaps in book 3 of a series.

Another special form of the Ally is the Seeming Ally.

In the world of archetypes, the Seeming Ally is called the Shapeshifter.

The shapeshifter comes in two forms: 1] The trusted character who is actually working for the antagonist. 2] The character that no one trusts who is actually very trustworthy.

Only Form 1] can function as an Ally.

Form 2] can become an ally much later in the story, after strong proof of trustworthiness occurs. This transformation to ally often comes in a second or later book. Many writers will sacrifice the Form 2] SAlly instead of sacrificing the confidante. As a writer, for the necessary emotional impact on the reader, you must clearly develop SAlly[2] in a quandary for not receiving the deserved trust.

In writing, your SAlly[1] is more important than the confidante. This character is devious and manipulative, caring nothing for the protagonist's honor or goals. Invest a little time in the 7 Deadly Sins when considering this character's motivations.

You may want to research the cunning and calculating sociopath if you are seeking a strong villainous character in addition to your antagonist. The sociopath would undermine your protagonist until the protagonist finally realizes the truth about SAlly[1].

Writing Goal for the SAlly

Again, remember the starting 7 before you work out the following.

1. When will the Seeming Ally turn on the protagonist?
2. What first reason will the SAlly give as justification for the betrayal? What is the real reason?
3. Is the SAlly going against the protagonist on his/her own? Or is the SAlly working for the antagonist and has been so working all along?

8 :: 2 ~ FOILS AND OBSTACLES

These characters play important roles in your story. While they usually are not strong secondaries, they do not belong in the tertiary rank.

Mirror, Mirror

Foils are characters who mirror the protagonist and proceed along that same path only to fail, often tragically. They foreshadow what may happen to the protagonist if s/he does not make the dynamic changes necessary. We meet foils early, and usually their *end* result occurs before the midpoint of the book.

Foils reflect one or several of the personality traits of the protagonist. These are the characters who can be associated with the protagonist then killed off to create a suspenseful belief in the audience that the protagonist will be killed off as well.

You can have more than one foil. In *Romeo and Juliet*, Shakespeare had four for Romeo: Mercutio, Benvolio, Paris, and Tybalt.

- Mercutio had Romeo's wit and extreme happiness when things worked well. Acts I and II would have little humor without Mercutio, and his Queen Mab speech, about dreams that turn into nightmares, foreshadows the tragedy of the play. Thus, Shakespeare uses him to keep the audience engaged as well as introduce a primary motif. Mercutio dies at the beginning of Act III, which is the center of the play.
- While Benvolio was not a strong character, he represented Romeo's sober side as well as his fairness: Benvolio enters the play at the very beginning, in opposition to Tybalt. He attempts to stop the fight between the servants of the Montagues and Capulets, a clear display of his willingness to obey Prince Escalus' law. However, when challenged by Tybalt, Benvolio will not back down from a fight. Benvolio disappears from the play at Act III.
- Count Paris is the worthy suitor for Juliet, good-looking and wealthy, related to Prince Escalus, and charming. Unfortunately, she met and fell in love with Romeo first. Paris represents the enduring love for Juliet, for he brings flowers nightly to her tomb after her supposed death. To exhibit enduring love, Paris appears in the play's last act—before he's killed by Romeo. (While Romeo is one of the protagonists, he is also the only character who commits two murders as well as causes the death of his best friend. Shakespeare lays five deaths at his feet, including his mother's and Juliet's.)
- Tybalt, with his unreasoning despising of all things Montague, represents that famous line by Friar Laurence: "These violent delights have violent ends." His need for revenge drives Acts II and III, just as Romeo's unreasoning need for revenge drives him to kill Tybalt after Mercutio is killed.

Foils highlight the protagonist's weakness or flaw. They cannot withstand the trial that undermines their weakness. Thus, their failure helps the protagonists prepare for their own test. This is the lesson that Aragorn learns after Boromir's struggle against the Ring in *The Fellowship of the Ring*.

The protagonist's dynamic changes are tied to three major discoveries: the desired goal rather than end result, the betrayal of the SAlly, and the true heart of the antagonist. Learning these three clarifies the nobler path of the protagonist. Otherwise, s/he is merely a foil.

So, what are the roles of the foil?

1. To present characteristics of the protagonist's personality.
2. To present a motif of the play (Mercutio and the Queen Mab speech).
3. To increase the strength of the protagonist by displaying the foil's weakness.
4. To foreshadow a possible end for the protagonist.

Writing Goal for the Foil

While you do not have to consider all of the starting 7 (e.g., goal, stressor, zenith), you may wish to consider how each of your foils will present one of the four roles, especially #4. To build to that point, do look at the starting 7 and decide which one of those will create a crucial moment for the foil as well as for your protagonist.

Creating foils for the antagonist can be intriguing, but how many characters are you going to give to your antagonist? Never let the page-count for the antagonist overwhelm the amount you devote to the protagonist. Otherwise, the antagonist begins to become the protagonist for your novel.

Concrete Walls

Blocking Figures are tertiary characters who cause obstacles that the protagonist must overcome.

Since I used *Romeo & Juliet* for the foils discussion, I'll talk about Juliet's blocking figures here.

First, Juliet is blocked by her parents' wish to marry her off to someone of wealth and higher status. Her parents carefully selected someone that they thought she would wish to marry. While some performances of the play present Count Paris as much older, Shakespeare's lines tell us that he is only a little older than Romeo. He is young and handsome, related to the ruler of their city, and wealthy.

When Juliet pretends to comply with her father's edict that she acquiesce to the marriage to Count Paris, her father moves the wedding up on her, necessitating her drinking the potion that causes her death-like sleep much earlier than planned.

Count Paris, while a foil to Romeo, can also be considered a blocking figure for Juliet. Her parents are pushing for her marriage to Paris, and she will become a bigamist if she goes through with the ceremony. Paris' pursuit of Juliet sets the clock ticking toward the end of the play. She cannot remain in Verona and wait on Romeo's return from Mantua or she will break the laws of man. Paris is just attentive enough and charming enough that she recognizes him as a danger to her heart's connection to Romeo—and her fear is that he will cause her to break her heart's lawful connection to Romeo. Juliet and we the audience see Paris' solicitude of her when they encounter each other as he is leaving Friar Laurence's cell (yet another similarity to Romeo, also tutored by the friar).

A third blocking figure for Juliet is her nurse, who begins as her confidante, proved when she carries the message to Romeo in Act II. When catastrophe occurs in Act III, the nurse advises that Juliet marry Count Paris, even though she would be committing bigamy. The ally-nature of the nurse is destroyed in this scene.

Blocking figures are especially strong when they are family or close friends of the protagonist. They get in the way, for the best intentions. Love and guilt are strong motivators for the protagonist.

Well-intentioned family and friends often see the protagonist on a different path than the one that should be chosen. For this reason, they will actively block the protagonist from the desired goal.

Additional blocking figures can be employers who force the protagonist to choose between livelihood (job) and a mere promise of a relationship. Mentors and counselors in the role of confidante (but not truly a confidante) can steer the protagonist away from the desired goal. The goal often seems unreasoning, impossible, a dream easily shattered. The protagonist's determination in continuing with the goal shows inner strength and moral courage.

These characters can supply guilt as the protagonist is pulled between the old, easy path and the newer, challenging path that leads to the Dear Desire.

Writing Goal for the Blocking Figures

Blocking figures belong in the third rank of characters for your novel. As such, you can paint them in broad strokes, just as you would any **stereotype**. However, because you may refer to them at several points in your novel, do list their specific details of appearance, work, and services as a blocker in your **Master Book**.

Pull your blocking figures from the protagonist's close circles of family, friends, job, and guidance.

- Who can you place between the goal and the protagonist?
- Who will tweak the protagonist's guilt?
- What rights will the blocking figures have to manipulate them emotionally?
- What strengths will the blocking figures have that will make the protagonist doubt the goal?

8 :: 3 ~ Two Additional Side Characters

Before we leave the secondary rank of characters, those who are strongly attached to the protagonist through emotions or a team role, we need to look at the Love Interest and the Trickster.

Love Interest

In many stories of the Quest, Monster, or Voyage and Return, the love interest is reduced to nothing more than a signifier. Often, LI was merely the woman beloved by the protagonist. Writers would walk the LI into the story, proof that the protagonist had a heart and had something to come home to. Brief mentions of the LI would keep her in the audience's mind. After everything was over, the protagonist came home, welcomed with open arms by a woman who never asked what had happened.

The above description is the process used in many action-adventure movies and comic books. If the female LI had any involvement in the story, she served as an item in jeopardy that had to be rescued by the hero (who wasn't truly a protagonist). The Iron Man series has broken this mold with the character of Pepper, more so in the latter movies than in the first one. Pepper begins as an unrequited LI; however, she still has to be "fixed" at the end of the third story.

Raiders of the Lost Ark developed the Love Interest into an ally. Marion Ravenwood is depicted as a strong and independent woman. As she and Indy run across the airstrip, escaping from the Nazis, they are hand-in-hand and running stride-for-stride.

More recent action-adventure stories cast the love interest as a man with the woman as the protagonist. However, that flip of gender does not remove the LI from the total Side Character role. To change the Love Interest, create that person—male or female—as a member of the team. Lindsay Buroker does this very successfully in her Emperor's Edge series.

Trickster

The trickster character thinks himself clever, but his actions only cause problems for everyone else.

A famous Navaho myth of Coyote is the perfect example of the trickster. Coyote gets involved in many different actions, some which work out to the good and some which do not. Going in, Coyote doesn't have expectations that his actions will cause problems; he just wants to be "doing". His intent is neither benevolent or malevolent. He just wants things to happen.

Coyote recognizes the power of the Old Man (a representative for God) that is so much greater than his own power. In this respect, he comprehends the limitations of his own abilities. But he still has fun.

Puck in Shakespeare's *Midsummer Night's Dream* is a trickster much like Coyote. His pranks are not born in malice although people may be emotionally hurt. He understands and obeys the authority of Oberon, but he may walk the edge of a sword in adding a little bit of fun to his obedience.

Loki of Norse myth has been called a trickster. He's not. He's a shapeshifter. He pretends to be helpful to Odin and Thor and the other Aesir, yet his purpose is to undermine them. He pretends to help the Aesir only to switch sides and help the giants, playing both sides. His pretense is born in malice, for he hates the Aesir. He also hates the giants. He cares only for himself. Since he cannot have the rule that he wants, he works to undermine all authority around him. Eventually, they see him for what he is and imprison him, with the venom of a serpent dripping upon him.

Odysseus is a true trickster. He is clever. He devises ways to outwit people instead of only resorting to strength or authority.

When he and his men are trapped in a cave by the cyclops Polyphemus, he comes up with a way to help his men escape rather than be eaten. He also blinds the monster to ensure their escape. Enraged at being blinded and losing his dinner, the cyclops chucks boulders around, hoping to injure the men who escaped him.

After the escape from Polyphemus, Odysseus reveals his arrogance about being clever. Pride drives him to tell the cyclops who blinded him. In doing so, he gives the cyclops a direction to aim the boulders—and nearly sinks the ship they are escaping on. The cyclops prays to his ancestor Poseidon to punish Odysseus; Poseidon does so.

Of course, Odysseus is best known for the Trojan horse, the ultimate trick that requires multiple steps: convincing the Trojans to pull the horse into the city, hiding quietly until the whole city is asleep, then sneaking out and opening the city gates for the conquering Greeks.

Odysseus is a clever idiot. While he can use brute force and military skill, it's his intellect that helps him devise his traps and the escapes from other traps. As idiot, he must arrogantly ensure everyone knows he is clever. That's a simplistic explanation for trickster.

If you use a trickster in your novel, remember that the character can be a prankster. Tricksters like Coyote and Puck have fun with their pranks, and only they would think of those pranks. Neither considers the effects that will result from those pranks. They enjoy the chaos.

Odysseus understands the necessity of order over chaos. He is representative of the clever prankster in an authority position, the tricks controlled to have an outcome beneficial to the side that he is on. Yet he still makes mistakes, for he doesn't fully consider the consequences of his actions.

Pranks. Fun. Cleverness. Chaos. No thought of consequences. These are the five traits required of every trickster character.

8 :: 4 ~ WALK-ONS & CAMEOS

Walk-on characters provide information or do minor errands. They are often hangers-on who have a single purpose. In this respect, you can consider them stereotypes.

Walk-ons should not take an active role and interfere with the protagonist as the main character.

Cameos are characters you want to highlight, especially if they are important characters in previous books or in books to come. Since they are significant, you can use them again as a blocking figure, a foil, a confidante, an ally, or even a SAlly (as long as the Cameo remains true to the personality you created for him previously).

4 Roles to be Filled

- Threshold Guardian ~ determined to block the protagonist's passage but once defeated will step aside and present no more difficulties.
- Idol ~ the character that the protagonist has looked up to but who is revealed as having clay feet.
- Herald ~ comes onto stage to deliver important information then leaves, job done.
- Jokester ~ This is not the Trickster. The jokester plays to an audience. He doesn't care about being witty or smart. He doesn't care about devising snares or escapes from snares. He will joke at the lowest level possible. He doesn't care about the audience's derision, as long as he is getting laughter. Clever tricksters do care about their audience's reactions; they want the adulation. A jokester's actions are actually reactions, a cyclical feeding off his audience.

8 :: 5 ~ MINIONS OF EVIL

5 Simple Opponents

We see these simple opponents most often because they are easy to set up and knock down. They will function very well as minions, representatives of a powerful antagonist. For shorter or simpler stories, they can serve as the antagonist.

Villain ~ over-the-top bad guy. The classic example is Snidely Whiplash in *the Dudley Do-right* cartoons.

Straw Man ~ a character set up as a one-sided evil who is easy to defeat. *The Devil wears Prada*

Bully ~ the stereotypical bully who tries to intimidate those who are weaker. When confronted, the bully runs away like a coward. *The Karate Kid*

Beast ~ large and dangerous. Feared because the primary motivation is animal-based. The beast usually lacks human mercy because the sole focus is food. Think of the beast as a predator hunting its prey. *Jaws* or *The Grey*

Alien ~ the off-world stranger, with unknown strengths and motivations, unknown weaknesses and reactions. *Alien* or *Predator*.

5 Not-Simple Opponents

Most writers do not write these not-simple evil-doers as they truly are. They back off once the story gets going. When writers do follow through, we readers and audience get a memorable story that others try and try to imitate.

The Corrupted ~ This character no longer behaves in expected ways but is driven by some inner perversion, usually of relationships or of motivation. *Anatomy of a Murder* presented a psychopathic murderer and his girlfriend. *Whatever Happened to Baby Jane?* was a warped narcissist who could not move past the time when she was idolized, decades previously.

The Femme Fatale ~ *Basic Instinct*. An alternative to this is the **Black Widow**, who kills the opposite sex for personal gain, whether that is monetary or an intrinsic goal not easily understood.

The Mastermind ~ *Terminator*. Relentless, clever, constantly adapting and learning, and determined to bring the opponent down.

The Criminal ~ Moriarty in the new *Sherlock* series. The criminal abides by the rules set for and by her/himself. All social and governmental rules can and will be broken.

The Disturbed ~ *Hannibal*. While the criminal is interested in breaking institutional rules, the disturbed will break the most basic rules. We have a great abhorrence of cannibalism; the disturbed is fascinated by what others consider an abomination.

. ~ . ~ . ~ .

Of course, the best opponent seems not to be an opponent at all ~ **the Perfect Person** ~ Mary Crawford in the 2007 *Mansfield Park*.

WEEKS 9 & 10 :: ENVISION YOUR WRITING

For the next two weeks, you will be writing every day.

For the past eight weeks, you have sketched the basics for characters and plot. Then you shaped them into rough forms.

Now it's time to draft.

After drafting comes revision (which is not re-writing the story. It's fixing and adding and removing). Once you have proofreading and corrections completed, you will publish.

We still have a little bit of plot shaping to finalize, but we're going to draft in a strong two-week start to our novel.

LAUNCH INTO WRITING

Dwight V. Swain in *Techniques of the Selling Writer* explains that books are made up of **scenes and sequels**.

Every scene has five points (derived from the **7-Point Plot**, used by Algis Budrys at the Clarion Writing Workshop):

1. A character
2. in a setting (or situation)
3. must have a problem.
4. The character tries to solve the problem
5. but fails to do so and in failing makes the problem worse.

Sequels are the bridges between the scenes. They are hardest to write. Sequels create the flow. Without them, the reader is jerked through the book.

In the scene, the primary viewpoint character is active. In the sequel, that character considers what has occurred, considers the current position in the continuing situation, and considers potential paths to move ahead toward the goal.

The sequel provides the launch into the next scene. A chapter can be a long scene followed by its sequel or multiple scenes/sequels.

The character is your viewpoint character, whether that is your protagonist, the antagonist, or another primary or secondary character.

A Word on Viewpoints

Only three basic viewpoints exist for story-telling. You will find various names for these, including "deep point of view". The classic terms are these:

A. Objective: no characters' thoughts or feelings are presented. Only outward behaviors, actions, and reactions are seen. Sometimes described as "whatever a fly on the wall would see". Objective viewpoint prevents empathy with characters.

B. Omniscient: the thoughts and feelings of multiple characters are presented throughout the novel. This is deep point of view with more than one character presenting a viewpoint. Most novels use omniscient, even if they are only telling the viewpoints of two characters.

C. Limited: the thoughts and feelings of only one character are presented throughout the novel.

Since we're on viewpoint, I'll give you a **major No-No**: Don't head-hop in a scene. Head-hopping is jumping from the thoughts/feelings of one character and into another character's head. You can do this, but you have to change scenes first.

Most readers also do not like to read a scene which isthen re-told from another character's viewpoint. Yes, you want to get across what each are thinking. Why not do that for separate scenes?

Omniscient viewpoint in a novel allows you to show character growth, which the Objective does not and which sounds arrogant in the Limited viewpoint.

So, if you have more than one viewpoint character, the first thing you need to determine when launching into the draft is which character will tell the first scene.

The number of scenes/sequels for primary characters should outnumber those for secondary characters.

.~.~.~.

If you have no idea how to start writing the novel, here are 3 options to help you start:

Opening Option 1

Walk the primary viewpoint character into the scene. Describe the situation then the setting. Give that character's attitude about both. Then roll into the action.

Alternative A to Option 1

Begin with a secondary character (whose viewpoint will recur consistently throughout the book). Beginning with a secondary character allows you to present special characteristics of the protagonist without the protagonist appearing arrogant.

Alternative B to Option 1

Begin with the antagonist, exhibiting all the evil you have invested into the character.

This opening is a classic for a book about a murderer or a serial killer.

Even if the antagonist does not provide viewpoint scenes/sequels in the book, you can open with this. You will need to remain in the Objective Viewpoint if you are not presenting the scene from a non-viewpoint character.

Option 2

Begin with the dominant symbolic image for the entire book. Present the image objectively, as anyone would see it. Then walk in the protagonist or another character. Present that character's opinion of the symbol.

Option 3

Begin with a highly active event—in objective viewpoint—the end of which brings the primary viewpoint character into the story.

A Word on Openings

No matter which option you chose for an opening, you need to insert a question in the reader's mind.

- Who is this person?
- How can s/he be stopped? OR How can s/he stop this horrible event?
- Why is s/he doing this?
- Why does it keep getting worse?
- Who is helping this person? This is especially effective when an antagonist has a minion. The minion is stopped, then an action occurs that is clearly caused by someone else. When this happens, the reader knows the problem is not limited to one enemy. Whether this is an action-adventure with an explosion or a literary novel where a person's venom is blocked only to have an unknown person cause more conflict among seemingly similar people in the neighborhood or workplace, this method starts many novels.

I have seen several writing rules for openings, including "Don't start with the weather." True.

Start with the viewpoint character experiencing the weather. Give that character's opinion of the weather.

Reader engagement occurs emotionally. Either readers need to empathize with the characters, be intrigued, or be horrified.

Three things attract a reader to a book: the cover, the blurb (back copy or sale copy), and the opening sentence.

The opening sentence is our focus now. You may not get the first sentence exactly right just now. Start with something. As you draft the book, keep looking for the best opening just as you looked for the best tagline to center the book.

Sample Opening Sentences

In these samples, look at how many use opposition or unusual circumstances. Also look at how simple many of these sentences appear.

Barbara Hambly, *The Silicon Mage* :: "The worst thing about knowing that Gary Fairchild had been dead for a month was seeing him every day at work."

Mary Stewart, *My Brother Michael* :: "*Nothing ever happens to me.* / I wrote the words slowly, looked at them for a moment with a little sigh, then put my ballpoint pen down on the little café table and rummaged in my handbag for a cigarette."

Mary Stewart, *The Gabriel Hounds* :: "I met him in the street called Straight."

Amy Tan, *The Joy Luck Club* :: "My father has asked me to be the fourth corner at the Joy Luck Club."

Daphne du Maurier, *Rebecca* :: "Last night I dreamt I went to Manderley again."

Stephen King, *The Gunslinger* :: "The man in black fled across the Desert, and the Gunslinger followed."

J.M. Barrie, *Peter and Wendy* :: "All children, except one, grow up."

William Goldman, *The Princess Bride* :: "This is my favorite book in all the world, though I have never read it."

Dodie Smith, *I Capture the Castle* :: "I write this sitting in the kitchen sink."

Ha Jin, *Waiting* :: "Every summer Lin Kong returned to Goose Village to divorce his wife ,Shuyu."

Victoria Holt, *Bride of Pendorric* :: "I often marveled after I went to Pendorric that one's existence could change so swiftly, so devastatingly."

Alice Walker, *The Color Purple* :: "You better not never tell nobody but God."

Graham Greene, *The End of the Affair* :: "A story has no beginning or end; arbitrarily one chooses that moment of experience from which to look back or from which to look ahead."

The Greene quotation, of course, is guidance for all writers. Our decisions are arbitrary.

Writing Rules

Whatever method or option or opening you arbitrarily choose, whether you write the first scene to tell your story chronologically, whether you jump to a major scene and construct the puzzle pieces of the great novel jigsaw, here are your writing rules.

- Begin.
- Write your best copy. Format correctly from the start. Keep everything organized.
- Have a clean draft. Tell the story that you would want to read.
- Avoid gaps in the scene and its sequel. Don't put in gobbledygook.

Writer's Block doesn't exist.

Many more professional writers than myself adhere to this philosophy.

You may have encountered on Pinterest or writing blogs such posts as "10 Types of Writer's Block and How to Overcome Them."

Here's the truth. Whether someone lists 10 types or 20 types or 7, they all fall into three broad categories: Refusal, Procrastination, and Inertia.

Refusal occurs when writers feel burnt out. They need to schedule a break or an escape. The creative brain needs to be re-charged, which can only happen if you take a day or two off.

Procrastination is born of fear: of failure or of rejection. We all want to be liked. We want our writing, the pourings of our heart, to be liked. We don't want to be ridiculed. So we put off our writing dreams because we don't want people to mock us or—worse!—not buy our writing. Get over those fears and just do it.

Inertia is either depression (not clinical depression, that's different) or stagnation. To fight depression, change your diet to avoid sugars and starches, increase your water intake, and start exercise (just walking is great). We give in to stagnation when we claim that we have to wait on the muse. We don't wait on inspiration; inspiration waits on us. Never refuse a challenge and seek out change to avoid slimy stagnation.

How do you overcome Writer's Block?

Write a sentence.

Then the next sentence that comes after that one. Then the next. And the next.

You may not like these sentences. You may want to rewrite them. Don't, not until the whole scene/sequel is finished. Let creativity flow. Never critique or correct your writing in the same session with creativity. That crosses the wires between the two sides of your brain.

The Writing Session

After glancing over your mapped scenes/sequels, start every session with a jot list of 7 items to accomplish.

As you draft, let the ideas pour out, whether handwriting or typing. Rewind from the rapid-flow to add in and fix things. Continue with the rapid-flow writing. When you wind down, rewind to add and fix. Then sink into the rapid-flow draft again. Dean Wesley Smith calls this cycling, a method he explains in *Writing into the Dark*, another excellent reference for your writing bookshelf. Rapid writing and cycling back through is the best method for starting any session's writing.

Save careful construction for the next stage, revision. During the two-week launch, we want to get sentences onto the page and turn those sentences into scenes and sequels.

Remember to follow the four writing rules.

Don't stop until you reach the day's goal, whether a page count or a word count.

End each session with a jot list for the next session. I usually have items left over from my start list.

Writing Goals

For this first week, set a session goal of 1,500 words. That's a little bit more than 5 typewritten pages of 285 words each.

1,500 words is three five-paragraph essays which you became used to writing in high school and college.

How many days a week that you will write is up to you. However, these first two weeks, as you get into the discipline of the draft, **reserve one day** for catch-up. If you don't need the catch-up time, you can blast past your goal.

Reserve a second day for brain rest and planning the upcoming week. The creative side of the brain will need the rest, so do take this day off. You can write Sat / Sun / Tues / Wed / Thurs / Fri and leave off Monday. Or take Sunday off. Or Friday night off.

Anticipate that all plans will change. Roll with the changes.

TWO-WEEK LAUNCH ~ WEEKS 9 AND 10

CHART FOR WEEK 9

DAY & DATE	# OF PAGES	# OF WORDS	SESSION TIME	BRIEF DESCRIPTION OF FOCUS INCLUDING PLANNING DAY
1				
2				
3				
4				
5				
6				
7				
TOTALS FOR THE WEEK				

Average this week's total word count with the total page count. ....

Transfer Total Words and Total Pages to the **Visioning** page, which precedes Week 6.

Increasing counts create a sense of accomplishment and reveal the power of persistence.

Calculating Words and Pages to Session Time helps determine if you are focused.

CHART FOR WEEK 10

DAY & DATE	# OF PAGES	# OF WORDS	SESSION TIME	BRIEF DESCRIPTION OF FOCUS INCLUDING PLANNING DAY
1				
2				
3				
4				
5				
6				
7				
TOTALS FOR THE WEEK				

Average this week's total word count with the total page count. …………………..

Transfer Total Words and Total Pages to the **Visioning** page, which precedes Week 6.

Increasing counts create a sense of accomplishment and reveal the power of persistence.

Calculating Words and Pages to Session Time helps determine if you are focused.

ANALYSIS

WEEK	FOCUS	START DATE	END DATE	HOURS SPENT	WORD COUNT	PAGE COUNT
11	ANALYZE THE WRITING					
12	ANALYZE THE STORY A					
13	ANALYZE STORY B PLUS					

Total Number of Hours Spent :: ....

Total Word Count for Analysis :: ....

Total Page Count for Analysis :: ....

When you draft the story, the beginning ideas in this section
called **Analyze the Story** may change and even transform.
Story is organic and fluid; let it grow and flow.

FOR THOSE WORKING WITH THE E-BOOK VERSION, CREATE YOUR OWN TEMPLATE OF THE MAJOR CHARTS

OR DOWNLOAD THEM FROM WWW.WRITERSINKSERVI.COM WEBSITE, UNDER THE PRO WRITER ADVICE PAGE.

WEEKS 11, 12 & 13 :: ANALYSIS

In the next three weeks you will analyze the writing you've accomplished. The idea of *Me as Writer* is extremely important. It's not enough to dream; you have to believe. To believe, you take the opening steps to turn dream into reality.

Self-analysis is extremely difficult. It's an excellent tool for a writer to have, but most writers don't start understanding themselves until they examine the motivations of characters.

Taking a *vision of self* and turning it into a *reality of self*, that's hard. It requires commitment, devotion, and not everyone is willing to sacrifice immediate, short-term wants for a postponed dream.

We'll look at the Writing Self as well as the Writing Location. And then we'll take the most important step of all: We'll analyze your story, where you are and where you're going. Not just the Plot 7, but all the scenes and sequels that form the entire book will be blocked out.

If you believe you have a good handle on your story, you can skip these three weeks and jump straight to **Big Push Writing**. You can always return. If you run into a problem and can't decipher what is wrong, return to these three weeks for help.

- At an early point in your writing career, you need to identify the kind of writer you are as well as the basics of the space you use, the focus of Week 11. Before you hop over, do skim the material for Week 11. Understanding how your brain works when in creative flow is crucial to your writing future.
- Weeks 12 and 13 offer the significance of the 12 major stages of every story. Whenever I encounter a roadblock or need to cross an idea barrier, I remind myself of these principle stages.
- Week 13 also offers guidance for the important search for a cover designer as well as how to set word-count deadlines for the upcoming **Big Push Writing**.

As you work through these three weeks, continue to record hours spent and word counts, even when developing ideas rather than actually writing manuscript pages. Monitoring your time and recording word investment provides proof of what you're accomplishing.

Never delete what you develop. If you decide to trash it on Wednesday, by Friday you may want it back. If the trash decision does stand, you can use the ideas to seed a different book. Store it in an ideas folder for later books. If you change your decision, those trashed ideas are easy to recover.

11 :: 1 ~ ANALYZE THE WRITING

In the past two weeks and the preceding nine, you learned a great deal about your writing self.

Discipline

Did you maintain every writing day of the **Two-Week Launch**?

- Yes? Excellent! You can maintain the schedule when no disruptions occur. That's self-discipline.
- No? Why not?
    - Did you fritter away the time? Then you are not serious about writing and publishing. That happens, and having spent my time in frittering flutter-bys, I will tell you that a lot of story seeds can be pollinated then. But you are *not* truly serious, not yet. You can be. You have to decide to be so.
    - Did life keep interfering? That happens, always, even when we have the best intentions. We can't give three hours or even an hour and a half. Maybe we can manage a half-hour. I've been here, too. Thirty minutes is better than Zero. Leave your writing out, organized and ready, so set-up doesn't take precious minutes from that half-hour.
    - Did you choose to do something else? Watch Netflix or a movie? Sit on the couch and play games on your phone? When you remembered, you might have said, "I'll write when this is over." Ah, but you continued to the next? Consider your choices. Is this writing dream not important to you?
    - In the pressures of the day, did you just forget? Put a sticky note at a clearly visible place to remind you.

Method

You can learn a great deal from your approach to the preceding nine weeks.

- Did you work through every step, piece by piece, following the methods I provided? For example, did you use the whole Plot 7? You're a **Plotter**. Writers like Jeffrey Deaver know every step before they write the first sentence of their draft.
- If you found the whole process irritating and just skipped and started writing, you're a **Pantster**. Pro writers like Dean Wesley Smith, a major proponent of intuitive writing, would hate this entire book.

The methodical process offers great comfort. To abandon the methodical process offers great comfort. Those two contradictory statements are equally valid. The key is to find the writing method that works for you—and abandon that method when it's not working.

Plotter, Pantster, both: the classification doesn't matter. Writing each book will be different. Whatever brings the words pouring onto the page, this is all that matters.

Sequence

- Are you starting at the first scene then writing forward? You're Chronological or Storyteller.
- Are you picking and choosing the scenes/sequels that you write? You're a Puzzler or a Mosaic.

Here's the problems with Pantsters and Puzzlers: When they pick a scene here or there, they gradually have to rewrite to make the scenes fit together.

The problem with Plotters and Chronos is that they tackle the hard without skipping, which means they have to slog on even when tired.

Chronos and Pantsters are more intuitive, writing the story without requiring a map, discovering as they go. (Yes, I mixed the types. We're all individuals, fitted together in different ways.) Puzzlers and Plotters need definite ideas about the whole story before they start; their process is more logical than instinctive.

We can create columns of advantages and disadvantages for each method and sequence. You know what? With enough thought, the columns are of equal length.

If you start writing one way and want to change, do so. It's your writing. Only you know what suits you best.

Analyze

Classify your method and sequence.

Plotter or Pantster :	Reason :
Chronos or Puzzler :	Reason :

Consider your Discipline.

How did you use the 14 days?
You were to write 10 or 12 of those days. How many writing days did you achieve?
What interfered?
What did you allow to interfere?
Which days did you use for Rest / Planning / Creativity?

List the days that you missed.	
How could you have written for a half-hour or even 15 minutes on these days?	
What stopped you?	

Advice

Don't castigate yourself. Vow to do better. Discover how to do better. And move on.

II :: 2 ~ DETERMINE YOUR WRITING SELF

Who will you be as a writer?

Yes, I know we all want to be best-selling authors, on the New York Times list, with our books made into films, and newbie and wannabe writers anxious to breathe the rarefied air around us.

Let's get to daily reality.

Will you use your own name or a pen name?

This simple question has double-sided options. Luckily, we don't have to walk the keen edge of a sword blade for our answer.

Many writers want to use their own name. They want no hassles about real name vs. pen name, and they work to create a brand based on their own name. Those who have an especially unusual name find that it helps distinguish them from other writers—and readers buy the author name once they glom through a series that they love.

A great many writers use a variety of their own names. They might use initials with their surname or convert their first name to an initial and append their middle name which is only a slight alteration. Some writers use their maiden name rather than their current married name.

Yet in these days of cyber transparency, a great number of writers are using pen names to create a wall between their private lives and their public writing lives.

Most writers choose a pseudonym at the beginning of their career in order to avoid problems at their workplace, whether that comes from a boss looking over their shoulder for work product or untactful colleagues or more.

A few writers are working in a genre that might raise the eyebrows of those around them.

Others do not want personal information about themselves and their families and children out for rabid fans to locate. It's one thing to talk with fans at a book-signing and quite another to have them knock on the front door.

Wisdom tells us to build a wall between our private and our writing spheres. The thickness of that wall is your decision. You can create a glass wall or double-sided concrete.

Using a pen name also gives introverts a role to enact when they attend seminars and conferences and book signings.

Pseudonyms require careful selection. Certain genres call for connotative names. While Nora Roberts became famous for her contemporary romances, she chose J.D. Robb for her science fiction detective thrillers. J.D. Robb has a harder edge than Nora Roberts.

Salvatore Albert Lombino had a very successful career as Ed McBain and Evan Hunter. Study these two pen names. While the genre is the same, the subgenres are not. That subtle difference is reflected in these pen names.

Among Dean Koontz's pen names are David Axton, Leigh Nichols, and Brian Coffey. Notice the different sounds and emotions attached to all four of these names.

Barbara Mertz wrote as Barbara Michaels and Elizabeth Peters. The Michaels books are similar to vintage gothic romances;. The Peters books have a snarky heroine and an Edwardian setting; these books morph over time to become thriller epics.

Elizabeth Pargeter wrote historical novels under her own name and her Cadfael Medieval mysteries under Ellis Peters.

Victoria Holt, Jean Plaidy, Phillipa Carr, Eleanor Burford, Elbur Ford, Kathleen Kellow, Anna Percival, and Ellalice Tate had the real name of Eleanor Hibbert. That's 8 pen names.

- Under her own name, she wrote nine epics which were never accepted for publication.
- As Eleanor Burford (using her maiden name), she published 31 novels in a twenty-year period.
- She then turned to historical fiction, chose the Plaidy name for the books based on a location near her home, and in the course of her career penned 91 novels as well as several that were non-fiction. She sold over 14 million books under this pen name.
- As Elbur Ford, she wrote four additional novels; as Kellow, eight; and as Tate, five more.
- I count for her 24 titles under Phillipa Carr, her third most successful pen name, selling right at 3 million books.
- She only published one novel as Anna Percival.
- Her most successful pen name, however, was the one that I first encountered: Victoria Holt. She penned 37 novels under this name and sold over 56 million copies of her books.

Obviously, Eleanor Hibbert reveals the reason many traditionally published authors turned to pen names: they were prolific. Hibbert certainly was. Wikipedia has a lovely chart which tells us that her total number of books is 191. > https://en.wikipedia.org/wiki/Eleanor_Hibbert Two of her pen names were suggested by her agent at the time; one pen name was suggested by her publisher.

Hibbert called herself a compulsive writer, writing every day of the week, 5,000 words in the five hours before noon. In a typical month, she typed (on a typewriter, which she hated) 150,000 words (5,000 x 30 days). By the end of the year, she would have generated 1.8 million words.

She began publishing in 1941. Her last book was published in 1993, the year of her death. That's a fifty-two-year career. Even considering that her output might have been slower at the beginning and end of her writing career, she would have produced over 81 million words in 45 of those years.

In her afternoons, she proofread her own manuscripts, conducted research (essential for her Plaidy and Tate books), and answered fan mail. Evenings were for social pursuits and entertainment, with chess being her game of choice.

Go to Wikipedia. Read Eleanor Hibbert's biography. Of her own characters, she said, that her heroines are "women of integrity and strong character . . . struggling for liberation, fighting for their own survival."[6] While she did eventually bow to the changing dictates of the marketplace, Hibbert's earlier Holt and Plaidy books continue to be re-printed and sold in greater quantities than many modern writers can hope for. Many of her 48 books under other pen names are being reprinted under the Plaidy name.

As for pen names ~

Hibbert and Koontz and Lombino and others are proof that there's no dishonor in a pen name.

Look on your pen name as your business name. And start looking at your writing as a business. You want it to generate money, don't you? Then treat it like a business.

Determine How to Become Prolific

Just like you, I've read criticisms of prolific writers, the chief of which is that the quality suffers. While later books are always better than the earlier ones, I will argue that Hibbert's quality matches up to any modern writer who can barely produce a single book in three or four years. Her plotting is clever—which you would expect from someone who enjoys chess.

And I want you to complete your novel in 52 weeks.

You *can* go faster. You have to *want* to go faster.

I'll never achieve Hibbert's writing or publishing success; I started publishing too late. Yet I can adopt as many of her writing habits as possible and increase my own output.

Many modern writers work at an increased rate of publication. They use several pen names to hide their output.

While you are struggling with the day job, you will have great difficulty reaching 5,000 words, 7 days a week. You might be lucky to reach 5,000 words a week. Soon, though, as you understand what you're doing and how you're doing it, you'll be going over 10,000 words a week—and then even higher.

Search for ways to increase your output.

Many writers laud dictation to reach 10,000 words in a writing session. They rarely discuss the time taken to fix errors of skipping or misunderstood words, of punctuation problems and problematic clichés, and of revising to cover in the plot holes and cover over the character discrepancies. Factor in the time for these six problems that occur with dictation. Now add the additional time that you will need to train yourself to dictate as well as the time needed to train the program to your accent and idiosyncrasies of language. If you can only reach 10,000 words in one session then fix problems for the rest of the week, are you achieving more? Maybe. It's one solution.

A second solution is my method. I handwrite the rough shape of my manuscript. This is not for everyone. Now, I've been around computers for more than three decades (yes, I know. I'm ancient). I know a lot about computers and word processing software. I know an extraordinary amount about composition; I taught it weekly for three of those decades.

---

[6] Wikipedia contributors. "Eleanor Hibbert." *Wikipedia, The Free Encyclopedia*. Wikipedia, The Free Encyclopedia, 6 Dec. 2018. Web. 12 Mar. 2019.

Why do I not use computers for my writing? Here I am , computer- and composition-savvy, and using longhand. Well, I know myself. I know that composing on computer (or laptop, in my case) leaves me open to back-up and correct or add in and the like. That works for any nonfiction writing, which is logical in its every part. But for fiction—no.

On the laptop, every time that I back up to correct or add in or fix, I turn on the **critical** side of my brain. That turns *off* the **creative**. Fiction is all about the creative. When I'm working on a novel's rough shape, that's the creative side of my brain. When I turn on the critical side, it takes time to get back to the creative side.

I know this. I've known it for years. Even so, a couple of years back I tried to do the creative on the laptop. I thought it would be faster. My experiment didn't work. My word output plummeted. As soon as I returned to pen/paper, it shot up. Even with my having to transfer the handwritten MS to the laptop, I still quadrupled my output the very month that I returned to the pattern I used when I first decided to become a professional writer, the summer between seventh and eighth grades.

I think faster with pen/paper. I don't know why. Forming the words with ink somehow turns on the creative, and the words come faster than I can write them.

After three decades of the daily input of work into some variety of computer software, the ordinary person would think that I would be faster electronically. I am a speedy typist. But I don't *create* faster. It's that critical brain.

I think that my handwritten manuscript is a lot like dictation software. I can write in the back seat of a car while on vacation. I can write when I'm stuck in an office, waiting for an appointment. In the time it would take the ordinary person to bring out their phone, unlock the screen, navigate to the right app, load it/find the write file and start, I've whipped out pen/paper, recorded my ideas and am flying onto the next page.

You can find various methods for getting the creative words onto any kind of page. Dictation works. Rapid-write works, which is the third method that I will advise people to use to increase their output.

In rapid-write, you type the words just as fast as you can, without fixing them, inputting them quickly, without corrections or editing. Then you jump back to the start of the rapid-write session and fill in what's missing. Sometimes you're merely inputting phrases or outlining the basics of a scene. You return to the rough ideas and shape them into the first draft of your manuscript.

The key is staying in the creative and avoiding the critical. Rapid-write occasionally works for me but not consistently. It's that dang *backspace* key.

Job 1.

Decide your writing name.

If you decide to go the self-publishing route, you may also wish to create your own publishing imprint with a business logo.

As your writing career continues, you may add more pen names, all under the publishing imprint.

If you decide later to abandon that pen name, you're not tied to it. You can re-launch with a new pen name. Once you've established the basic, you can then re-publish those earlier books just as traditionally published writers do, ~ "Stephen King writing as Richard Bachman".

Job 2.

Whatever you decide, you will need to file for a tax identification number or the appropriate revenue department that issues business numbers for tax purposes.

Tax ID numbers allow you to sell books to retail establishments (book stores!).

Job 3.

Create a business email that you can easily access. Start funneling writing emails to that address.

Job 4.

Order business cards with your name, business name, business email, and appropriate phone number.

Most purveyors of business cards offer hundreds of images for logo options. That logo can match to your business logo or be something else. Whatever you choose, keep in mind that you are taking the first step to build your author brand.

Blank backs allow you to write brief notes.

Writing begins to feel like a real profession when you hold your own business card. You'll get a tingle of excitement the first time that you hand your new biz card to someone.

Select your font, card appearance, images, and colors with an eye to the specific name with which you will start your writing career.

These four jobs will take time (and money). You might wonder if you would be better off writing?

WIBBOW = would I be better off writing? First coined by Scott William Carter, this is your essential question anytime that you step away from your writing desk.

Well, the answer is "Yes!" Resoundingly yes. Yet we can take time for the business side when we schedule these tasks during a writing lull, as we're doing this week before we go for the **Big Push**, 13 + 13 weeks of straight writing—half the year drafting your novel.

So get these jobs out of the way. Do your inspirational research on people like Eleanor Hibbert. If she's too intimidating, look up Phyllis A Whitney, a writer who's not as prolific but still a mighty seller who described herself as a writer of *romantic novels of suspense.*

Look at Salvatore Lombino, 90 books to his names. Look at his "Get in and Get It Done" essay that appeared in *The Writer* in 1978.

Look at Stephen King's output. Look at Dean Koontz. Look at Dean Wesley Smith and Kris Rusch. All prolific. All quality work.

All treating their writing as a business.

They know who their writing self is, and they work for their writing self.

You don't need to hire writers—then stiff them for their pay—to be a prolific writer. It's basically BiC, Bum in Chair.

The Writing Business

JOB 1	WRITING NAME	BUSINESS NAME
JOB 2	TAX ID FILING DATE RECEIVED DATE	TAX ID NUMBER
JOB 3	BUSINESS EMAIL SET UP	EMAIL ADDRESS PASSWORD
JOB 4	BUSINESS CARDS IMAGE CHOSEN COLORS FOR AUTHOR BRAND FONT CHOSEN BIZ TAGLINE	INFORMATION FILLED OUT BUSINESS CARDS ORDERED BUSINESS CARDS RECEIVED

FOR THOSE WORKING WITH THE E-BOOK VERSION, CREATE YOUR OWN TEMPLATE OF THE MAJOR CHARTS OR DOWNLOAD THEM FROM WWW.WRITERSINKSERVI.COM WEBSITE, UNDER THE PRO WRITER ADVICE PAGE.

11 :: 3 ~ Control Your Work Space and Habits

Do you have an area devoted to your writing? You should.

Set aside an area where you can work BiC. Yes, I know, you like the couch. Or spread out on your bed. Or your comfy chair. Or the kitchen table when everyone is gone.

Those won't work.

First, comfortable places are known BY YOUR BRAIN as comfortable places, intended for lazing around. And that's what your brain will do, laze and meander and drift off and be distractable.

Approaching your writing space will soon become habitual. The habit itself will affect your brain. It will turn on the writing synapses as you walk toward it.

Second, you can count your writing space as a tax deduction. Seriously. Measure it out and report it on your tax return. It's nice to have deductions when you have increasing income.

In your writing space, put what you need to generate ideas.

Essential Tools

- Tools for Writing: pens or pencils & paper / laptop & printer & paper / mouse & mousepad
- Tools to Save your Eyes: copy stand / sticky notes / highlighters / great lamp / magnification glasses / amber glasses to avoid blue light
- Tools to Save your Health: timer / sturdy tabletop / great chair / rolling wheels and chair mat

The amber glasses to avoid blue light and the magnification glasses will save your eyesight in the long term. Your eyes are the key to a long, prolific career.

The timer, especially a Pomodoro timer or its equivalent, reminds you to get up and move around, which is beneficial to your eyes and your body. Follow the 30/5 or 45/15 rule: work for the longer span; walk around for the shorter span. As you walk around, look at distant objects. You have been concentrating on a screen about an arm's-length from your eyes; rest your eyes by looking away.

BiC has its own problems. You need a great chair, one that supports your upper and lower back areas as well as your bum and hip joints.

Working in your lap, leaned back with your feet up sounds great, but most writers who do use that posture have reported problems with carpal tunnel syndrome. Save the kicked-back, relaxed time for when you are revising and proofreading. It's tedious work; you need to feel relaxed then.

- The seat should be adjustable. Lower it to prevent your legs dangling; raise it to prevent your legs from scrunching up your hip joints. You should not feel the seat braces that support the cushion.

- Having arms for the chair is up to you. The ability to lower and raise the arms should be an option.
- You do not need a head rest—that's turning the chair into a sleeping area, which defeats the purpose of the work space.
- Rolling capability cuts both ways; you need to roll to access things just a little way, but don't roll across the room. Get up and move. That promotes blood circulation, and blood feeds the brain, right?

Do you know who spends more time at a keyboard than writers? Professional pianists. What posture are they taught? What is the position of their hands in relation to the keyboard? What is the position of their legs under the keyboard?

- Additional Tools to Save Time: paperclips / binder clips, scissors, sticky flags, flash drives, paper for notes / foam board or cork board to post the sequence of the novel / calendar of upcoming goals / inspirational photos / calculator

Notice that I didn't add your smartphone. It's not in this list.

Smartphones are a huge distraction. It dings; you pick it up, disrupting your thought process. You know what? Messages can wait. Emails can wait. Notifications can wait.

What if it rings? Once again you pick it up and disrupt your thought process. Nope, let's not to this. You know what? Important calls will go to voice mail.

Do you pick it up for research? You know what? That can wait. Make a note of the research you need, and keep writing. After you finish or the next day before you start, find the information you need. Start the next session with inserting the information where it needs to be. Keep the internet away from your writing area.

About the only reason you should have the smartphone nearby—not close by—is for white noise. Background noise drowns out other people talking, cars passing, dogs barking, and the constant phone dings. Select something like rainfall or waves on the shore or quietly rhythmic music composed without words.

Songs you like to sing to are disruptive. You stop writing and start singing. In some books, writers have posted their writing song list—driving guitars, heavy drumbeats, singers screaming. Nyah, not conducive to creative flow, people. Natural sounds are tied to the creative flow.

Classical music is based on mathematics. That will turn on the critical side of the brain. We need the creative brain. Again, head for the natural sounds: waterfalls, rain, ocean waves, crackling fire.

As I mentioned earlier, we're talking about this now because you have two Big Pushes coming up. Handle the set-up now, in this break, not when you can't stand an issue any longer or you get stressed because the words aren't coming. If you have to stop and move things around, that turns to the critical side of the brain.

Nature. Comfort but not ease. Tools handy. Work space ready.

11 :: 4 ~ ANALYZE YOUR CALENDAR

Look back at the past 10 weeks. What disruptions kept you from completing the goals for each week?

Look ahead for the next 15 weeks. List your commitments.

1. Family always comes first.
2. Work pays the bills.
3. Health should never be neglected.
4. Social includes friends and close colleagues from work and other social activities like church.

These are the four necessities.

Anticipating what might interfere can help writers overcome the inevitable slow-downs from disruptions.

If you know a day will be spent driving to and from a family gathering, schedule that day of the week for your rest / planning / creativity day. Plan for the flip, and you'll glide through the week.

Family and Friends and Other Social Commitments

Relationships with family and friends and colleagues keep us going. All relationships are built on the tripod of attraction, compatibility, and devotion. Most important are the three bonds: the family bond, the friendship bond, and the intimacy bond. We work to maintain compatibility and devotion over the progress of years. If any leg of the tripod fails, then the relationship begins to falter.

Family is the strongest and most reliable bond.

You may have conflicts with family members. You may have past history to overcome. Only a few people are totally dysfunctional—deep into drug use, twisted by past traumas, sociopaths or psychopaths, or severely unbalanced through chemical deficiencies. Not all members of your family, however, have these problems that make them difficult to get along with. Most of your family are people that you can totally rely on, the ones who want the best for you, the ones who support your struggles.

We bond with friends who've suffered with us through trauma. The vast majority of our friends, though, are friends of association rather than true connection.

And you need to be aware that there are concentric circles of friendship, with the closest friends almost like family then working outward to those who are better than acquaintances but with whom we have no common background. Our bonded friends should be able to call upon us in times of trouble.

On the outer rim of our concentric circles of relationship are the friends of association, the new friends, the acquaintances—these are not the people who will sit with us day after day at the hospital. They might drop in, that's all. Bonded friends will be there without being asked.

Social commitments can be difficult to avoid. Remember **WIBBOW**.

Overcoming Guilt

Family and bonded friends impose the greatest guilt when we're tugged between them and our writing. When they need us but we're desperate for words, we have to release the writing goal. We can re-schedule or work harder.

And when we're with family and friends, we need to be totally present. Be engaged with them, not distracted by the smartphone. The rules for our writing business—no smartphone during creativity, calls can go to voicemail, texts can wait—these hold doubly with our strongest relationships. When you have been *with* them, then it's much easier to say "no" to them when you *need* to be writing.

As writers, we have to say "no".

- "No, I can't go to the movies this weekend. I went last weekend with you. I need writing time tonight." True friends and family will support your goal and be willing to re-schedule later.
- "No, I can't volunteer for that meeting. I volunteered last month and the month before."
- "No, I can't watch your baby all day Saturday. I'll be happy to watch him for two hours, but I can't give you the whole day. Yes, I love him, but I need time to concentrate on something."
- "No, I'm sorry. That's not possible. I have something that I really need to get done."

That last bullet point should work for all situations. It's polite. And they're rude if they inquire too closely. Just look at them. Don't say anything. Then smile and walk away.

And shift them farther out in your friendship—to the acquaintance concentric circle.

Work Pays the Bills

Keep the day job long after you want to write full time.

Don't write at work. The rabid boss who discovers you writing on the clock could claim your writing as work product and garnish your hard-earned writing dollars. That's a worst case scenario, to be sure, but don't become the example for it.

After all, as famous as Nora Roberts is, only fools would plagiarize from her—but it keeps happening, most recently with the #copypastecris scandal.

Work commitments can drive you crazy. When the boss demands four extra hours, which will interfere not only with your writing time but also your sleep time, your schedule is blown for two days, not just one.

And you can only work harder before the stress begins a mental and physical collapse.

If you've had a stressful week, sleep helps. Exercise helps. And both of those help your overall health.

Writing is Sedentary

Writing for hours after hours is not healthy. I wish it were.

BiC requires your body to sit at a desk, arms lifted, for long, long minutes. Even if you dictate while on a treadmill, you still need seat-time.

The Pomodoro method of 30/5 or 45/15 will help. Just keep moving during the writing breaks. Look into the distance.

Get a step tracker and try to increase your steps. A minimum of 10,000 per day is best.

Good eating habits are essential. Good nutrition feeds the body and the brain. Bad food sends it into decay. Avoid highly processed and overly sugared foods and drinks. Carbonation is not your friend.

Avoid caffeine when it will interfere with your sleep. Some people cut it completely. I love coffee too much.

Plenty of pure water is essential. Water is God's nectar. Spring water or distilled water should be your choice. 64 ounces is the minimum. It will also drive you to get up and move around.

Adequate sleep and sunlight affect your creativity and your mood. Writing depends on both of these.

Doldrums? Lethargy? Increase sleep and sunlight. If the problem doesn't fix itself in a day, drink more pure water. Purify your diet: no starches or sugars, no fast foods, no highly processed foods. Start walking. If you can't go 45 full minutes, do three sets of fifteen.

Fallen off the nutrition and the exercise? Start right back up. If you injured yourself, resume your regimen more slowly—geez, use a little common sense.

At the end of a week with all seven of these in action, you should see an improvement.

11 :: 5 ~ CHALLENGES TO OVERCOME

We dealt with a great number of the disruptions that will challenge your writing in **11 :: 3** and **11 :: 4**.

We can avoid most disruptions with adherence to a simple adage: Plan life to live life. Or Plan Writing to Live Writing.

Not all disruptions can be planned and flipped around. How will you overcome these?

Disrupted once or twice is easy to make up over a two-week span, using the Rest / Planning / Creativity days.

But when you've spent four solid days sitting with a friend in the hospital? Or you have an unplanned trip that you couldn't avoid? Your schedule is blown before you know it.

A contingency plan can help. Squeeze in an extra 30 minutes in the morning and 30 minutes at night. Cut outside interests for a month. Work harder and smarter. Stay focused and healthy.

Work harder by planning to use small increments of time. Dictate scenes into your phone while driving. You stay engaged in driving, more engaged than if you were texting someone. (*Never* do that, please!) Use every increment of time to rough out scenes and dialogue.

Work smarter by knowing what's coming next. Know what's coming next by planning. Be willing to dump the plan when the creative muse jumps into the story. The plan, however, will keep you on track.

Before you leave for work, read over what the next writing session will cover. Stumped? Quick-write some ideas, even foolish ones, right before you go to sleep. You may have the answer by morning. Even when it doesn't seem obvious, when you start writing, something will be there.

When you finish a writing session, jot your ideas for the next session. Start the next session by listing what you will write. No, don't read over the ending session list. *Write* this session's list. The simple act of forming letters will start your brain working.

And remember that you are drafting. Revision is to come. Write your draft as cleanly as possible, with no skipped scenes. If you don't like what you've written, let it stand. Tell the subconscious to work on it. Continue on. During revision, the fix will pop out. Such is the mystery of the subconscious, which works when we sleep and works when we aren't thinking about what it needs to do.

Waiting on Inspiration

Here's another adage to live by: Writers don't wait on inspiration; inspiration waits on us.

The creative muse hides behind the tree words and the rock sentences, in the caves of paragraphs and the pages of labyrinths. She'll jump out when you least expect her.

But you have to hunt for her. We hunt with words and sentences and paragraphs and pages. If you don't actively hunt her through your writing, she'll never surprise you with the best idea ever.

Don't whine about Writer's Block. Nope, I don't want to hear it. There's no such thing as Writer's Block. I'm not the only writer who claims this.

Look, we can always write words. They may not be "inspired". They may not be the words we want. They are words, however.

If your word flow on your project is obstructed, your two-sided brain is trying to tell you something.

- Go back and look at what you've written. Do you see a gaping plot hole? A character who needs flesh on his bones? Do you need to re-consider a setting? A twist or two?
- The way forward may be unclear. You can rapid-write the next few scenes then go back and build those. Or work on a different project entirely.
  - Sometimes I can mix my projects; usually I cannot. I can mix craft books and blogs and fiction, at whatever stage of the writing. I can mix revising/editing one fiction project while generating ideas and roughly shaping a second fiction project.
  - I cannot simultaneously shape or draft two fiction projects. Are you confusing your muse?

Writer's Block is never the answer to your problem. It's an unacceptable excuse. Burn that into your brain.

Before the two-week launch, I briefly mentioned how writers mis-identify their problems as Writer's Block. I spent a long chapter of *Think like a Pro* (book 1 of this series), explaining the three types of blocks and giving tips on how to overcome each. I offered creativity exercises that will prove you're not blocked—just as a text to a friend or an email to a work colleague proves it.

Don't believe me? Search it. Search for "no writer's block" and see what comes up. The Pro Writers, the ones constantly producing, the ones who should run out of ideas but never do—like Salvatore Lombino or Eleanor Hibbert or Dean Koontz or Phyllis Whitney—they don't blame Writer's Block. They just get on with the writing.

You should as well.

WEEKS 12 & 13 :: ANALYZE YOUR STORY

If you just skim through the information for these two weeks, you're going to think it's too simple.

We're creating the structure of the entire book using the Archetypal Story Pattern, **ASP**.

You will have heard of Plot Points (with their pinches), the 7 Parts of a Story, Freytag's Pyramid, Aristotle's Dramatic Structure, and Shakespeare's Play Structure. You may have worked with *Skin the Cat*. You may have found a list of tropes common to your genre and are madly trying to figure out how to put each one into your novel.

Stop. Just stop. Tropes don't build a story. Tropes *enhance* a scene.

The **Archetypal Story Pattern** has been used since prehistoric man sat around a fire and entertained listeners with stories of the day's hunt. Every myth of the occidental cultures follows **ASP**; many of the oriental cultures use the same pattern. The fairy tales of our childhood align with the 12 stages of **ASP**.

Blocking every major scene based on the **ASP** helps the writer in you comprehend the interlocking parts.

If you want to write a good story, use **ASP**. Devote a pattern to each primary, especially if you have double protagonists. For a strong, constantly interacting antagonist, you will have three patterns. You may decide to cut some scenes as you go along. That's your choice as you draft. You still need to plan for them. Don't forgot the lessons of **11 :: 4** and **11 :: 5**.

Many books have been written about **ASP**, also known as the hero's journey or the hero's story arc. Joseph Campbell's monomyth (in his examination *Hero with a Thousand Faces*) delves deeply into the pattern from which **ASP** is taken. The book that's most accessible for writers is Christopher Vogler's *The Writer's Journey*. Both works draw from Carl Jung's work on archetypes, and Carl Jung must have been dependent on George Frazer's *The Golden Bough*. My teen-aged self seriously tried to read *The Bough* before giving up. I highly recommend Vogler's work for your reference shelf. Campbell's book, maybe.

Your work for the next week and a half will be to work through **ASP**, blocking scenes for each stage.

You've generated ideas for each stage. Those ideas are on your tack board. Match these ideas to the **ASP** stages.

For each stage you'll find the bare bones meaning. The explanation will look simplistic. It's not. Read each sentence carefully. Understand how to apply each part of the arc's explanation to the character.

Remember. You are creating an **ASP** arc for each primary character.

To know *where* you are in the long length of the novel gives you the encouragement needed to finish. Even when you feel mucked-up to your knees, you can see what needs to happen and commit to driving through the mire.

I do want to encourage you with the reminder that not all writing days are mucky mire. Most are pure joy. Celebrate those days.

You have developed the major points already, during the Plot 7, and quite a number of notes. Place the individual scenes of the Plot 7 at the appropriate stages of your story.

Scene blocking will be a guide, but your creative muse can venture off on a new trail. When you stray too far from the path, you can return to these trail blazes that will steady your venturing.

Over-planning, especially if you robotically follow this ASP guide, can chain your muse. Be willing to abandon everything and just write. Strangely enough, the pre-blocked scenes will morph into something better, as if your subconscious mulled them over to improve them. Without pre-blocking, however, the subconscious can't work.

Good luck. Only it's not luck, is it? Happy trails as you follow these blazes through the novel backcountry to reach your own completed story.

12 & 13 A~ ANALYZE THE STORY

For each stage, consider which will fit your original vision of the story through the Plot 7, worked out in Weeks 3 and 4

Separation & Departure

The opening triad stages of the **ASP** belong to the story segment of **Separation & Departure**. The primary character is forced to leave the "home". After **Separation**, s/he is often filled with simmering hostility or burgeoning anxiety long into the middle stages. **Departures** are never undertaken lightly. No hints exist to reveal whether return is imminent or even possible. Fatalistic characters expect doom. Rosy idealists blur reality until the blinders are ripped away. Optimist, pessimist, or realist cynic, all will drive against the obstacles beyond the loss of hope.

1 ~ Ordinary World

OW starts with the first moment of trouble, the first moment when Normal skews off-direction. Often called the Narrative Hook, the **OW** opens with the Normal so readers will understand the extent of the disruption.

The disruption will lead to the protagonist's transformation. If you start with the antagonist, consider the **OW** that s/he wants and is acting to cause.

2 ~ Call to Adventure

In the **C2A**, a deep-seated personality trait will drive your character to step away from the crowd and seek the adventure. Whether Protector/Defender, a Trickster, or a Shadow element unforeseen until this moment, this trait will motivate your character to react to the disruption of the **OW**.

Dynamic characters act when everyone around them either waits passively or reacts unthinkingly.

Originality in your story starts with your opening sentence. The **C2A** seals your commitment to offer a story worth the reader's monetary and time investment.

3 ~ Refusal of the Call

RoC, born in the **C2A**, portends the character's isolation from the home group of the **OW**. The trait that drove the **C2A** reaction also drives the **RoC**. No one seeks true isolation from the people who offer love and a sense of belonging[7].

The character could not prevent her/his reaction in **C2A** but can valiantly fight the consequences.

The ancient Greek philosopher Aristotle first understood that true protagonists become isolated

---

[7] Maslow's Hierarchy of Needs

from those around them. Isolation causes mistakes in logical thinking. Love and belonging needs can only be fulfilled for people by people. Pets can partly fulfill the need but not wholly.

The opening triad gives a glimmer of the true conflict. The protagonist confronts the first obstacle. The sacrifice of something dear (usually an illusory desire) is necessary to drive any character into willful isolation.

Initiation / Descent and Departure

View the middle six stages as two triads. The first three form the Initiation; the second three are the Descent & Departure.

Initiation determines if the character is worthy enough for this venture. Many are *not* worthy; they lack what the business world calls the soft skills: reliability and efficiency, diligence, problem-solving, presence when needed, ability to communicate and work with others, adaptability and creativity, and leadership. These 10 soft skills often determine long-term success.

The protagonist has these skills or quickly learns them; this sets her/him apart from the many who are not worthy.

The **Descent** is the life-threatening venture, whether that threatened life is physical, professional, or psychological (remember, James Scott Bell).

In the rush to the next stages, writers often neglect the **Departure**. How will the character cope with isolation and difficulties? Anticipation never meets reality. We are more than physical beings. Delve into the emotional, intellectual, and spiritual spheres of the character.

The **Departure** is as figurative as it is literal. The protagonist leaves the old perspective and starts the venture into a new one. Whether the change comes through an actual journey or a metaphysical quest undertaken while still at home, the protagonist leaves the old desired dear—now destroyed—and pursues the destruction of the dear's destroyer.

4 ~ Meeting with the Mentor

MwM starts the six stages that form the bulk of the **ASP** and the bulk of any story. You can have a lot of fun with the different kinds of mentors. Here are just 10.

- Guiding Sybil
- Riddling Oracle
- Scary Crone
- Wizened Wizard
- Mysterious Hermit
- Insane Recluse
- Fanatic Prophet
- Skilled Veteran
- Aged Sage
- Wounded Expert

The mentor's advice can be confusing, working in symbolic metaphors or multi-part complexity. A mentor can teach or serve as a font of wisdom when joining the adventure. Those whose simplistic advice might be dismissed will eventually be discovered as wisely prescient.

5 ~ Crossing the First Threshold

While the opening conflict merely hinted at the antagonist, in this fifth stage of **X1stT** the true conflict is now comprehended as so much more than anticipated. Whether through the early sacrifice of the illusory desired dear or a comprehension that no one else could confront the struggles, the protagonist continues on through the **X1stT**. This understanding comes after the reactive encounter with the antagonist. From this point on, the protagonist must become active.

6 ~ Tests, Allies, and Enemies

Seemingly simple, **TAE** covers a massive amount of ground. When story drags through sloggy slime, readers may abandon it and never return.

Originality drives **TAE**. Deliver the most creativity in this extended stage. Through betrayals and shapeshifters (always holding the chiefest of these in reserve), surprises to characters, plot twists and unexpected consequences, feints and ripostes, the tests will gradually unveil allies and enemies.

Avoid alternating sequences. Not all enemies are minions of the antagonist.

Confirming allies is as important as discovering enemies.

Between the **TAE** and the **AIC** is the center of the **ASP**, but in the book it's the 60% mark.

7 ~ Approach to the Inmost Cave

The Inmost Cave is the lair of the antagonist. Discovering its location is as difficult as the approach to it.

Caves are guarded in unexpected ways, and the guaranteed assault on those who approach will hit at the four layers of the individual: physical (first layer), intellectual, emotional, and spiritual (deepest). The death of a loved one is a greater struggle than healing after a physical injury. An assault that exploits doubts is more wrenching than the collapse of a well-crafted plan.

8 ~ The Ordeal

Also known as the Dark Moment, the **Ordeal** is the 75% mark of any novel.

Here is the long-awaited *mano y mano* battle between the protagonist and the antagonist. The Darkness is the lack of hope for the primary character going into the battle.

The protagonist is sustained by those same skills and allies and lessons learned since the **MwM**, but those skills and allies and lessons mean nothing against the antagonist. What keeps this character still strong, still struggling even when overwhelming odds should crush? The answer is the very personality trait introduced in the **OW**.

Imprisonment is a type of escape because it delays death.

9 ~ The Reward

In the **Ordeal**, we left the character in extremities. The ninth stage, the **Reward**, is the unexpected save, for a true Dear Desire replaces the illusory one sacrificed at the **C2A**.

Whether the protagonist stumbles upon the means of escape or remembers the seemingly insignificant detail (given by a misunderstood mentor? Or a shapeshifter form[2]?) that cripples or kills the antagonist, the **Reward** allows the venture to proceed with success.

Nothing is ever again as dark as the **Ordeal**.

Return and Re-Integration

The final triad of the **ASP** reveals the transformation of the protagonist. The antagonist remains static. Should the protagonist not return to the **OW**, we the readers would not truly comprehend those changes.

Re-Integration requires that the protagonist with allies and the true Dear Desire return to their **OW** to resume their normal existence. In this, we see how someone ordinary conquered an extraordinary challenge. The characters do not return to their former behaviors: too much change has occurred. Yet we readers want to anticipate life beyond the novel's pages.

10 ~ The Road Back

The antagonist may not have been defeated at Stages 8 and 9, although s/he can seem to be so defeated. The brighter that the **Road Back** is, the darker the next stage will be.

The **Road Back** is still packed with trials, twists, and betrayals. In the Plot 7, the betrayal can occur before the **Ordeal**, during it, or here at the tenth stage. What would keep a hidden shapeshifter waiting to reveal her/his true purpose until after the antagonist is seemingly defeated?

The protagonist is weakened by betrayal. A sudden defeat will allow the resurrected antagonist in the next stage to threaten the protagonist one last time.

11 ~ The Resurrection of Evil

We're at the 85-90% mark of the novel.

The antagonist might return. A strong minion who could potentially become an even stronger antagonist could challenge the protagonist. An undefeated shapeshifter (revealed in Stage 10, dealt with in this stage) could assault your primary character. Whatever evil is resurrected, its attack is surprising, ruthlessly shocking, and merciless. The last deaths occur here, and not just of the forces of antagonism.

12 ~ Return with the Elixir

An **Elixir** is the restorative potion of the gods. It's better than nectar, which is the gods' usual drink. This stage proves the protagonist is extraordinary, even though s/he will seem as ordinary as before.

Triumph has two effects—arrogance and humility. People who win by chance become arrogant because they believe Fate is on their side, with a juggernaut of success attending them. People who struggle to overcome understand the cost, and they know how thinly edged is the sword that cuts victory from defeat.

A printable ASP Chart follows the chart to use for Big Push the 1st.

For those working with the e-book version, create your own template of the major charts or download them from www.writersinkservi.com website, under the Pro Writer Advice page.

FINISHING WEEK 13 B ~ ANALYZE YOUR NOVEL'S PRESENTATION

Finally! Yes! We're talking about cover designers and deadlines.

The first 10 days of Weeks 12 and 13 drained your creative impulses as you struggled to link all the scenes together, focusing on original ideas as much as possible. Wisdom says to let the critical side of your brain have playtime. Otherwise, the critical will pop out when you least want it to do so.

Designers

If you are going for traditional publication, I wish you all the best. This step is not for you.

However, if you will indie publish, this step is extremely important. Readers see your cover first; good covers will entice readers to take second and third looks at your novel.

You could risk making your own cover. The operative word is *risk*. Do you understand balance and proportion? Symmetry and juxtaposition? Chiaroscuro? You do? Then you've had a bit of artistic training.

Graphic designers working in indie publishing understand how to blend different elements while keeping the various layers of the images in balance and proportion. They understand when color saturation is a good thing—and when it can overwhelm. They understand when embellishments work and when to subtract the embellishments. They understand how font choices can disrupt the whole synergy of image and title.

Do you understand all of those?

I don't. And I don't want to take the time from my writing to figure it out.

That's actually the question to ask: Would I be better off writing? WIBBOW.

If you decide to find a cover designer, you start with scanning the published books in the genre and subgenre to which your novel will belong.

Ask these questions:

- What catches your eye?
- What doesn't?
- What dominant images do you see over and over and over? (Like the running girl in a red coat, the ubiquitous cover for a couple of years.)
- What kinds of dominant (foreground) images do you like?
- What fonts do you like? Which ones do you hate?
- What is the ratio of image to font? Is the title blasted over the cover? Is that what you want?
- Check the small thumbnails on the online stores. Which covers attract the eye? Which covers look amateurish? Which covers stand out?

- Study the designer's use of chiaroscuro. What is the light source? How are the shadows working?
- How does the designer use the font choices? The best designers will use similar fonts for the title, series name, and author name.

If the book offers sample pages or you can find the print edition in a bookstore, look on the back of the copyright page or in the acknowledgements by the author for the cover designer.

You can run a google search for book cover designers. Many designers offer inexpensive pre-made covers. On the designers' websites, you should be able to see their portfolio of work for hire.

Once you have generated a hot list of the top 5 designers, get into the nitty gritty information.

- Price ranges for covers (this will sometimes make the decision for you)
- Price ranges for social media packages (you need this for promotions)
- Price ranges for the addition of paperback covers
- Limitations on your use of the cover image
- Designers' creation of branded covers for other authors (in their portfolio). Branded covers have a common look across all the books in a series.
- Lead time for scheduling. (You are at minimum 26 weeks from completion of your novel. That's eight months. You could possibly finish sooner. You will know at the end of the 1st Big Push, 13 weeks from now.) A long lead time gives you an opportunity to save up for a better cover designer. ($20.00 once a week is a meal and dessert x 13 weeks = 260.00. You can give up going out once a week, can't you?)

Once you've narrowed down your search to the top 3 designers, determine how you will pay for the cover and anything else that you purchase.

It's not wise to give out your credit card information, even if the designer has a lock in their URL that supposedly assures your personal information is safe. Millions worldwide use services similar to PayPal—and that's another consideration with your cover designer. Online payment services provide a guarantee for you and your designer, and the designer will not have to wait on banking laws for the money to be released to them.

When you set up the payment service, you provide personal and payment information, so be careful about the service that you select. You provide contact information, usually your email address and a phone number. More and more online retailers are using these payment services, so you can practice with known retailers before you connect with a cover designer.

Once the designer finishes the cover and receives your approval, the designer's office will send an invoice via the payment service to your email. You can click a link in the email to authorize payment, after which you will receive a payment receipt. Only then will come the package of images for which you contracted.

WORD COUNTS AND DEADLINES

Word-count deadlines work by the power of increments. Write a certain amount on a steady basis, and the total words in the project will escalate until you achieve completion.

- Anything at 40,000 words or more is considered a **novel**.
- A **novella** is 17,500 to 40,000 words.
- A **novelette** is 7,500 to 17,500 words.
- Anything under 7,500 is a **short story**.

To determine your word-count total, you need to know the standard length of a novel in your genre. Generally—and this is a big *generally*—word counts fall in these ranges and do not exceed 150,000.

The Adult Fiction Market:

- Trade Fiction (literary or commercial) ~ 90,000
- Historical Fiction ~ 100,000
- Mystery ~ 70,000 to 90,000
- Romance ~ 50,000 to 100,000
- Science Fiction / Fantasy ~ 90,000 to 120,000
- New Adult Fiction ~ 50,000 to 80,000

The Children's Fiction Market:

- Young Children's Picture Books ~ 32 pages
- Older Children's Picture Books ~ 48 pages
- Children's Chapter Books ~ 1,000 to 10,000 words
- Junior Fiction (Middle Grades) ~ 10,000 to 20,000 words
- Young Adult Fiction ~ 40,000 words or more

Now, determine the increment that you want to aim for as your goal: 50,000 or 70,000 or 90,000 or 100,000. Then divide into words per day, working five days a week.

We have 26 weeks to bring this novel's draft to completion. That's 5.9 months. You won't write every one of those days. Life happens. You get sick. Someone that you have to take care of gets sick. The boss makes you spend overtime. You get stressed. You have to pay bills and do taxes. You go on vacation because you're stressed. A dozen more things could happen.

So let's call those 26 weeks about 5 months.

Can you achieve 500 words a day? That's the five-paragraph essay for high school and early college, remember? In a 5-day week that's 2,500 words a week and 10,000 per month, which is 50,000 words in five months.

How about 700 words > 3,500 a week > 14,000 per month > 70,000 in five months.

For 90,000, 900 words each day > 4,500 a week > 18,000 per month..

Going for the Gold of 100,000 > 1,000 words in five days > 5,000 a week > 20,000 a month.

Just have to be extreme? 1,200 words over five days leads to 6,000 words per week and 24,000 per month for a grand total in five months of 120,000 words.

Here's the key: Work at your pace, not someone else's. You know how much life controls your writing time. Squeezing out 500 words daily is still an achievement.

Many new writers will advise you to dash through the draft, skipping the hard or boring parts. I can't stop you from doing this. Puzzlers and Mosaics write the parts they like, leaving the parts they don't like for the end. Skipping results in two problems:

1] Writing all the good leaves you facing only the bad. With only the bad before you, you will procrastinate. Chrono writers, those who write beginning to end, achieve goals faster because they don't procrastinate.

2] When you dash through and leave a sloppy mess filled with *scene needed here* or *something clever goes here*, you dread starting the clean-up. Write the best draft, beginning to end. A reasonable daily word count gives you the time needed to think through to clever scenes *and* helps you create clean copy.

Writing a clean copy first-time will eventually become habitual and cut down your prep work, which is always the goal. Like any craftsman builder of houses, we'll adjust as we go, nixing common design elements and replacing them with fresher ideas.

DRAFTING

WEEKS 14 TO 26

WEEK 27

WEEKS 28 TO 40

DRAFTING THE NOVEL ~ WEEKS 13 TO 26

In the charts for the series of the **Big Push** weeks, every one of the seven weekdays is listed. Always set aside one day for Rest / Planning / Creativity. Set aside the second day for the same, but you can also use it for catch-up.

Week numbers are not listed; that's for you to fill in. Both **Big Pushes**, weeks 14 to 26 and weeks 28 to 40, are 13 weeks of straight writing, totaling 26 weeks or half the year. You don't have to write every day, but you should attempt to reach your week's word-count goal.

FOR THOSE WORKING WITH THE E-BOOK VERSION, CREATE YOUR OWN TEMPLATE OF THE MAJOR CHARTS

OR DOWNLOAD THEM FROM WWW.WRITERSINKSERVI.COM WEBSITE, UNDER THE PRO WRITER ADVICE PAGE.

Here we go!

BIG PUSH THE 1ST ~ WEEK _____

13 WEEKS OF DRAFTING

WORD COUNTS

GOAL FOR THE WEEK :: _____

TOTAL FOR NOVEL :: _____   % OF TOTAL ACCOMPLISHED_____

DAY & DATE	# OF PAGES	# OF WORDS	SESSION TIME	BRIEF DESCRIPTION OF FOCUS INCLUDING PLANNING DAY
1				
2				
3				
4				
5				
6				
7				
TOTALS FOR THE WEEK				

ASP STAGE(S) WRITTEN ::

CHAPTER(S) WRITTEN ::

PAGE NUMBERS WRITTEN ::

TOTAL PAGES THUS FAR ::

TOTAL CHAPTERS THUS FAR ::

TOTAL WORD COUNT COMPLETED ::

WEEK _____ OF 13 (WEEKS 14 TO 26)

FOR THOSE WORKING WITH THE E-BOOK VERSION, CREATE YOUR OWN TEMPLATE OF THE MAJOR CHARTS

OR DOWNLOAD THEM FROM WWW.WRITERSINKSERVI.COM WEBSITE, UNDER THE PRO WRITER ADVICE PAGE.

ARCHETYPAL STORY PATTERN

ASP STAGE/ CHAP. #	POV CHARACTER	BRIEF DESCRIPTION OF SCENE	USE OF PLOT 7?
SEPARATION AND DEPARTURE			
OW			
C2A			
RoC			
INITIATION/DESCENT AND TRANSFORMATION			
MwM			
X1stT			
TAE			
AICave			
Ordeal			
Reward			
RETURN AND RE-INTEGRATION			
RdBck			
ResEv			
Elixir			

FOR THOSE WORKING WITH THE E-BOOK VERSION, CREATE YOUR OWN TEMPLATE OF THE MAJOR CHARTS

OR DOWNLOAD THEM FROM WWW.WRITERSINKSERVI.COM WEBSITE, UNDER THE PRO WRITER ADVICE PAGE.

THIS CHART, UNLIKE THE OTHERS, IS AN EXPANDABLE WORD DOCUMENT.

WEEK 27 ~ TAKE A BREAK

This week, take a vacation from active writing but not from your writing business. We're going to get everything we need

27 :: 1 ~ CONTRACT WITH DESIGNER

With Big Push the 2nd still ahead before you complete the draft of your novel, now is the time to schedule with the designer.

Count ahead 12 weeks. Send your email asking if the designer has availability around that date. Ask if the designer uses a template or questionnaire for the cover design information. Also ask when the designer would like to receive that design information.

The cover design template will confirm your genre and target audience. Professional cover designers are familiar with the standard covers for both.

Also on the template will be the book's atmospheric quality and the setting. Beyond a description of your primary characters, you might also point to colors and specific items that you want on the cover.

Most cover designers work with stock photos. If you browse around on ShutterStock or DepositPhotos or PeriodImages, you might find cover models that you can use. If you want a specific look for your cover models, you may have to contract with an illustrator. Once the illustrator provides you with an excellent quality digital image, you can forward that to the cover designer.

You will also need to create a synopsis of your novel, not only to give the designers the basic idea of the story but also for the back-cover copy.

You will not turn in the template to the cover designer at this point. That will occur close to the contracted date (which is the reason you need to know how far in advance of the contract date that your cover designer would like to receive the information). Most designers have a two- or three-week turn-around from receipt of the questionnaire to final cover design.

27 :: 2 ~ ISBN & COPYRIGHT

Every book that is sold worldwide has an International Standard Book Number. In the USofA, we purchase the ISBN from *Bowker*. In Great Britain, according to an internet search, is *Nielsen UK ISBN* agency. If you are in a different country, just search for ISBN and your country. A search for India turns up *Raja Rammohun Roy National Agency for ISBN*.

You will have to purchase separate ISBNs for each edition: one novel in ebook and print (paperback) editions means that you purchase two ISBNs.

While you cannot get a copyright on your novel until it is published, you can certainly explore the copyright agency for your country.

27 :: 3 TO 5

For the remainder of this week, read what you have drafted on your manuscript.

Print out your manuscript, and read the print-out. While you may be used to reading from a computer screen, you will discover that reading the print-out creates objective distance for you.

Read closely. Track any changes that are needed as well as ideas that need to come in—but do *not* make them yet on the computer. Sticky notes are excellent for these planned changes. I write on the manuscript itself—this is a draft, remember.

If you aren't reading for revision or editing, what should you be reading for?

- Ensure the flow of scene into sequel and sequel into the next scene.
- Check the logic of events so that no steps are missed.
- Mull over the explanations that characters give for actions that they take as well as motivations for those actions.
- If you've not yet done so, track the clues for the mystery or the clues that will lead to the antagonist as well as the ones that will reveal the shapeshifter(s).
- If you skipped and wrote "put something here" (even though I asked you not to do so), then fix these now.

Finishing Week 27 should mean that your book is half-written.

If you are ahead of the plan, EXCELLENT!

If you are behind the plan, what happened? Definitely explore the problems that you had.

Then do the necessary prep work for the coming 13 weeks: commitments, obligations, etc. Weeks 28 to 40 should **finish the draft.**

As you write, check over the changes and ideas that you developed for the first part of the draft. Which can you incorporate? Continue to note down the various clues. And don't *skip*!

BIG PUSH THE 2ND ~ WEEK _____

13 WEEKS OF DRAFTING

WORD COUNTS

GOAL FOR THE WEEK :: _____

TOTAL FOR NOVEL :: _____   % OF TOTAL ACCOMPLISHED_____

DAY & DATE	# OF PAGES	# OF WORDS	SESSION TIME	BRIEF DESCRIPTION OF FOCUS INCLUDING PLANNING DAY
1				
2				
3				
4				
5				
6				
7				
TOTALS FOR THE WEEK				

ASP STAGE(S) WRITTEN ::

CHAPTER(S) WRITTEN ::

PAGE NUMBERS WRITTEN ::

TOTAL PAGES THUS FAR ::

TOTAL CHAPTERS THUS FAR ::

TOTAL WORD COUNT COMPLETED ::

WEEK _____ OF 13 (WEEKS 28 TO 40)

FOR THOSE WORKING WITH THE E-BOOK VERSION, CREATE YOUR OWN TEMPLATE OF THE MAJOR CHARTS

OR DOWNLOAD THEM FROM WWW.WRITERSINKSERVI.COM WEBSITE, UNDER THE PRO WRITER ADVICE PAGE.

HARVEST

The harvest season gathers everything planted and readies it for storage. A writer's harvest celebrates that the growth part is over and completes the last jobs that will prepare a book for publication.

In writing, I work through 7 stages: sketch, rough shape, draft, revise, enhance, proof, and edit. When I've completed these, I can publish without hesitation.

The rough and the draft are the most brain-consuming. After I've finished these stages, I'm happy to turn to the critical job of revision.

WEEK 41 ~ 3 C'S WITH 4 D'S.

Celebrate! Tell people that you finished your draft. If they want to read it, say you expect to publish in ten weeks. Treat yourself to dinner at a fine restaurant. Completing your novel is the reason for the evening.

Cover Information needs to head to the **designer**! If you've not yet done so, write the blurb: A character in a situation encounters a problem. This problem will not be easily solved—why not? The situation should be unique; your tagline from Week 1 should be firmed up now and inserted as the opening hook. The blurb needs tight construction. Try to remain under 20 sentences. Proof and proof. Stay between 250-300 words.

Consider the whole manuscript. Rapid-read the entire thing as a print-out. Yes, I know you can read on the screen, but you need objective **distance**, provided by reading from the sheet of paper. The tactile nature of the printed manuscript creates a different mindset.

Place sticky notes where the story **drags**. Note any changes and additions. For example, as you read through the mentor stage, did you suddenly realize that your protagonist played the guitar? Where else in the novel can you briefly mention that?

Don't touch the manuscript other than these notes. Let it percolate a few days.

Definitely put a sticky note anywhere that you notice info dump is occurring. Info dump is the kiss of death (and so are clichés).

Weeks 42 & 43 ~ Revision

Now you can touch the manuscript. Complete the following in Week 42:

- Revise plot holes and character discrepancies.
- Tighten up your theme or tagline development. Touch back to the tagline or theme at least once per chapter.
- Look for places where the story events or character reactions are too predictable. You know the ones: you've seen those story lines and behaviors on TV. Avoid those.
  - How to be unpredictable? Kate Wilhelm's Law for originality will help here. The first thing you think of: toss it. Most people will think of that idea, too. The second thing, toss it, because many people will think of that. Only a few will think as far as a third thing. If you want to be totally original, you need to toss that third idea. The fourth, use it.
- You want to be ahead of the reader at the key points of your story (Plot 7). You want to be right with your reader throughout most of the story. Use the levels of Kate Wilhelm's Law to achieve this.
- Look for inconsistencies. Your Master Book should help maintain the same eye colors and character names and locales.
- Harder to spot are inconsistencies with character reactions. If you've created a certain behavior pattern for a character only to break it, your readers will not be happy. Perhaps you need that reaction to occur—does it have to come from that particular character? Would it be better as a reaction from a different point of view character?
- Which brings us to the viewpoint of each scene and sequel. Is the correct character narrating the scene? Would a different character allow more interesting motivations and opinions to be expressed?
- Does the story have slow downs because the pacing dragged? Or did the pacing speed through something you needed to spend a few more hundred words on.
- As you consider adding, also consider subtracting whatever is repeated more than three times or what was overkill for description or a scene you loved but which really doesn't develop the story.

After you finish your revising, over the weekend, hand the manuscript to a brutally honest reader who will look for these same issues and place another sticky. Give this reader a clean manuscript, not one that you've written all over. You need the MS back quickly, so make them sit down and read it in one sitting.

They'll hate you for that. Might make their critique more brutal. Isn't that a good thing?

In Week 43, get all of these revisions into the manuscript.

HARVEST CHARTS FOR WEEKS 41 TO 43

WEEK	FOCUS	JOBS		START	PROOF	COMPLETED
41	COVER	1] TEMPLATE COMPLETED 2] BLURB WRITTEN 3] SEND TO DESIGNER				
				START DATE	END DATE	COMPLETED
	RAPID-READ					
				START AND END DATES	NEW WORDS COUNT	PAGES REVISED
42	REVISION	DAY 1	CHAPTERS COVERED			
		DAY 2	CHAPTERS COVERED			
		DAY 3	CHAPTERS COVERED			
		DAY 4	CHAPTERS COVERED			
		DAY 5	CHAPTERS COVERED			
		DAY 6	CHAPTERS COVERED			
		DAY 7	CHAPTERS COVERED			

BRUTAL CRITIQUE ?

FOR THOSE WORKING WITH THE E-BOOK VERSION, CREATE YOUR OWN TEMPLATE OF THE MAJOR CHARTS OR DOWNLOAD THEM FROM WWW.WRITERSINKSERVI.COM WEBSITE, UNDER THE PRO WRITER ADVICE PAGE.

REVISION ~ WEEK 43

DAY 1		CHAPTERS COVERED
DAY 2		CHAPTERS COVERED
DAY 3		CHAPTERS COVERED
DAY 4		CHAPTERS COVERED
DAY 5		CHAPTERS COVERED
DAY 6		CHAPTERS COVERED
DAY 7		CHAPTERS COVERS

WEEK 44 ~ ENHANCE

You may have the cover back from the designer. Post it somewhere that you can see it for inspiration as the grunt work of revision continues.

You may still be working on Weeks 42 and 43. You'll have to double-down if you are.

To enhance something is intensify or increase the quality of something. In films, characters and certain locations often have musical motifs associated with them. You might want to associate a symbolic motif with each of your primaries. Do so also with your chief locations.

How do you pick a symbolic motif? Check out a list of common archetypes and symbols. You can find several different lists with an easy search. As you scan through, keep your characters and locations in mind.

- If you have a character who is always reticent to speak up, associate that person with different kinds of walls. Their words could be blocked, like water building behind a dam, or their words could tumble out slowly, like rocks dislodged from a wall.
- If you have a location where trouble always occurs, associate it with a square cage that imprisons. For example, you can describe the bars of shadow created by the venetian blinds when the sunlight pours in through the window.

In my book *The Key for Spies*, I associated a crow with one of the antagonists. In every viewpoint scene for him, I referenced a crow, a black bird, black wings, a cawing cry, or the like. I only mentioned this symbolic motif once per scene related in his perspective.

Look only at your descriptions ~ primary characters and locations. I might dip into a significant secondary character, but I wouldn't work deeper into the character list.

Limit your use of the symbolic motif. Don't extend it, or it can turn into a running joke.

Enhance

Week 44	Notes / Chapters Covered	Hours Spent	New Words Count	Page Count
Day 1				
Day 2				
Day 3				
Day 4				
Day 5				
Day 6				
Day 7				

For those working with the e-book version, create your own template of the major charts or download them from www.writersinkservi.com website, under the Pro Writer Advice page.

WEEK 45 ~ SENTENCE CRAFT

As we did with symbolic motifs to enhance descriptions, you can use sentence craft to improve your writing.

And as we did with the motifs, we need to limit any sentence craft. While some metaphors and symbols might crop up on every page, limit the ones that you deliberately craft to add. Keep these to every fifth manuscript page.

Sentence craft is the use of the major 7 types of figurative language: similes, metaphors (direct and implied), symbols, personification, apostrophe, hyperbole, and understatement. It also includes such rhetorical devices as chiasmus or auxesis. I've listed 7 below along with examples.

Most people are familiar with the common figures of speech. Only students who had great composition teachers will have heard of the rhetorical devices.

In addition to descriptions, you can easily work sentence craft into dialogue: "You know, Jacky, in that presentation Mike was soaring like an eagle until Alice brought up the failure at Plant 57." ~ **simile**

The use of "crop up" in the second paragraph of this section is an implied metaphor.

Finding examples of sentence craft is a simple matter of looking for rhetorical devices. Try "rhetoric and style" in the search box. ThoughtCo and Silva Rhetoricae have great sites; ThoughtCo is more accessible for novices to sentence craft. Easily useable for the writer are these seven: anaphora, antithesis, alliteration, polysyndeton, auxesis, zeugma, and chiasmus.

Anaphora: "**This** royal throne of kings, **this** sceptred isle, / **This** earth of majesty, **This** seat of Mars, / **This** other Eden, demi-paradise" (II i) ~ Shakespeare's *Richard II*

Antithesis: "It can't be **wrong** if it feels so **right**." ~ Debbie Boone

Alliteration: "The way to **d**usty **d**eath" ~ from Macbeth's famous speech by Shakespeare and the title of a book by Alistair MacLean

Polysyndeton: "It is acceptable to have no illusions—**and** safe—**and** profitable—**and** dull." ~ *Lord Jim* by Joseph Conrad

Auxesis: "Grind. Crush. Burn." ~ *Medea*, as translated by Robinson Jeffers. An ascending list of methods to kill.

Zeugma: "You held your breath and the door for me." ~ Alanis Morrisette or this example from *The Things They Carried* by Tim O'Brien: "He carried a strobe light and the responsibility for the lives of his men." The zeugma uses one verb for two objects, (one concrete and the other abstract).

Chiasmus: "You forget what you want to remember, and you remember what you want to forget." *The Road*, by Cormac McCarthy

WEEK 45 ~ SENTENCE CRAFT

LITERARY DEVICES	NOTES ABOUT USE	TALLY TO PREVENT OVER-USE	
		CHAPTERS WHERE USED	PAGES WHERE USED
SIMILE			
METAPHOR			
SYMBOLS			
PERSONIFICATION			
APOSTROPHE			
HYPERBOLE			
UNDERSTATEMENT			
ANAPHORA			
ANTITHESIS			
ALLITERATION			
POLYSYNDETON			
AUXESIS			
ZEUGMA			
CHIASMUS			

FOR THOSE WORKING WITH THE E-BOOK VERSION, CREATE YOUR OWN TEMPLATE OF THE MAJOR CHARTS

OR DOWNLOAD THEM FROM WWW.WRITERSINKSERVI.COM WEBSITE, UNDER THE PRO WRITER ADVICE PAGE.

WEEK 46 ~ TAKE A BREAK FROM THIS BOOK

We need more objective distance. We need to forget the scenes and sequels, the pages, the paragraphs, and the very sentences that we have spent so much time with. When we come back, we'll be **Finishing**.

So break away now. Throw this book completely out of your head.

How? Start writing your next book. See if you can complete Weeks 1 & 2 & 3 in one week. If the second book is a sequel to this one, this week should fly.

FINISHING

We set up our book's reach into the world at large. Next we have a last run-through for the novel, finding errors and correcting them. Then we publish!

COMPLETION CHART

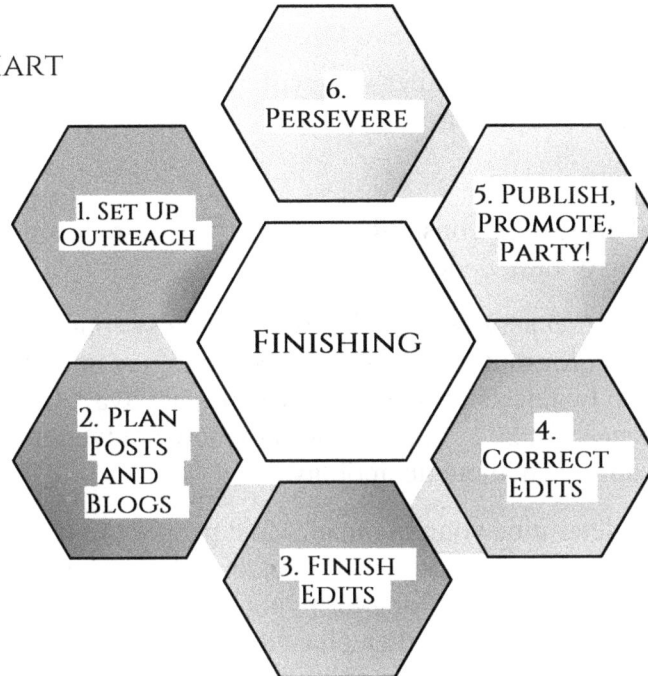

6.
PERSEVERE

1. SET UP
OUTREACH

5. PUBLISH,
PROMOTE,
PARTY!

FINISHING

2. PLAN
POSTS
AND
BLOGS

4.
CORRECT
EDITS

3. FINISH
EDITS

FOR THOSE WORKING WITH THE E-BOOK VERSION, CREATE YOUR OWN TEMPLATE OF THE MAJOR CHARTS

OR DOWNLOAD THEM FROM WWW.WRITERSINKSERVI.COM WEBSITE, UNDER THE PRO WRITER ADVICE PAGE.

WEEK 47 ~ SET UP YOUR OUTREACH

Job 1

Create an account with the online retailer who will distribute your book, whether that is Amazon kdp or Kobo or another distributor.

Job 2

Set up your website. This is time-consuming yet relatively simple since options abound that do not require an understanding of html code.

1st Step, find an ISP, internet service provider, who will host your website. Several great deals are offered when you contract for multiple years as opposed to just one year. Ease of use and ease of access should be your top two decision-makers. Free sites are available—but they could easily become pay-to-play in the near future . . . and if you somehow inadvertently offend the owners of the ISP, your whole site vanishes without an apology.

Your second step is to determine your site map. Most people use the standard offered pages: 1] landing page or front page, 2] blog, 3] about us, 4] contact us, and 5] one extra. Decide if you want to use this map or create your own. Think long-term, not immediately. If you plan to write three different series or in three different genres, then change the focus of pages 3, 4 and 5. You can convert your landing page into your blog page or a pillar page.

Pillar pages list the various topics for blogs, like an indexed table of contents based on categories. Some people convert the landing page into a pillar page and maintain the blog page.

Steps 3 & 4 ~ Once you determine your site map, you can select a theme, choose fonts, and determine a layout. Only after these are developed will you layer in your information.

Starting information to have:

- A website banner, which your cover designer could provide if you contracted for it.
- Cover image for your book
- Blurb
- Short biography
- Contact form
- Your professional email address
- A teaser for your next book

Job 3

Determine what other social media sites you will use. It can take a full morning to set up a month's worth of posts for a single website on one social media site. Use the social media sites that you always follow.

You should be able to create business pages off your personal account page. These pages will always be linked, and your readers will be able to track your personal life through them. If you want a thick concrete wall between the public and the personal, then you can open a separate account, but you will need separate emails, phone numbers, and possibly separate mailing addresses. If you start now associating certain emails and phone numbers and addresses (as well as credit cards) with your writing business, that soon becomes an easy flip for your brain.

Job 4

Make a video trailer using your blurb and cover images. You can purchase additional stock photos from online retailers such as ShutterStock and DepositPhotos. Sound images are available from like AudioJungle. You can use powerpoint to create a great trailer if you don't want to drop $$$ and spend hours learning a vastly different program.

Abide by the copyright for the images and music, just as you want people to abide by your copyright.

To use your video trailer as a promotion on social media sites and your own website, you should open a youtube account. (It just requires more and more, doesn't it?) Open the account in the name of your professional business.

Once the trailer is made, upload it to youtube. Use the youtube hyperlink on your website: it will automatically load in your video trailer.

And keep an accounting of your costs for stock photos and sound files. These are marketing and promotional costs that you can count on your taxes.

WEEK 48 ~ PLAN POSTS FOR YOUR OUTREACH

We're on a three-week count-down for publication.

Schedule the following 7 posts for the week of your release. Yes, you can schedule posts on your website and Facebook. As your starting date, use the date that is two days after you plan to upload your book to your online retailer of choice.

The extra two days are needed for the online retailer to finish approval and for you to get your link and check that everything looks the way that you want it to look. You will need to return and edit to add the link to each post.

Here are a week's worth of ideas for posts, for your website and for Facebook or other social media accounts. For FB and the social media accounts, you can use your cover image as well as the link directly to your online retailer or to your blog page which will also contain the link to the online retailer.

1. Announce the release with the release date. This post can be your inaugural post for your sites as well as your personal page. Use your personal page to direct friends and family to your business page.
2. Tease with the cover.
3. Blurb and cover image
4. Inspiration for book ~ You can use public domain images or purchased images.
5. Free first chapter
6. Favorite character scene or a similar teaser
7. Video trailer—based on the blurb and cover image, created last week.

You may want to blow your budget on ads. Wait. Wait until you have three books. Then promote the first book, which should passively drive sales to your second and third.

WEEKS 49 AND 50 ~ EDIT AND CORRECT

A line edit will look for typographical errors. Start at the back of your book, and read each page backwards. Be careful. Take your time. Take breaks. Don't be distracted by other things.

No one is 100% perfect. You may want to have another friend read behind you—or hire a local English teacher and give them a nominal fee.

Some people contract out this line edit (proofreading). You need someone with a massive vocabulary and better than usual punctuation skills. That's all.

`You can hire a local high school or community college English teacher for much less money than an "official" editor. The local teacher may be less likely to ruin your writing voice than an outside editor. Whoever you contract with—if anyone at all—tell them that all you need is basic grammar and typographical errors.

If you plan to contract out this work because you're shaky on your grammar, then flip this step with **Week 46**.

Please don't trust the computer grammar and spelling checker. It will not catch everything. It lets "vial troll" pass when it should be "vile troll".

Thank the friend who helps you now *and* the one who gave you the brutal critique *and* anyone else who has helped you on your Acknowledgements page, usually preceding the first page of the book (before your *Dramatis Personae,* if you have one).

WEEK 51 ~ PUBLISH, PROMOTE, AND PARTY

When you publish, use your ISBN.

When you click the final button to put your book on sale, sit back and breathe slowly. Then jump up with glee. It's *done*!

The online retailer will send an email telling you when your book goes live. At this point, you can create an author page for the online retailer and claim your book. This may take a couple of days (one for approval of the author page, the second for the book to be able to be linked). Use the link as you edit your social media posts.

From your author page, you can connect the RSS feed from your website blog. (Don't worry too much about this unless and until you start posting blogs at least once a week.)

Once your novel is live on your online retailer, file for copyright with your government's copyright office. According to U.S. Copyright Law—and most nations abide by the same type of law—your book is protected as soon as you finish it. However, if you ever want to prosecute someone for copyright violation, you cannot do so unless you have registered your copyright officially. (Mailing it to yourself, the so-called "poor man's copyright", holds no weight in court.)

Contact your cover designer with the link to the online distributor, and thank them again for their work.

Tell family and friends. Post it on your personal page. Be proud. Do you know how many people say they want to write a book? Over half the people that you will tell about your book will add that they want to write a book.

Do you know how many people participate in and *win* NaNoWriMo? 19%. How many of those winners ever publish? Much less than 1%. The most recent statistics are for 2010, which listed over 200,000 people as participants since the start in 1999. Over 600 books have been published in one form or other since 2006. That's 0.003% who have finished *and* published. You're joining an elite group.

Be proud of your accomplishment.

And plan to repeat it.

Check on your scheduled promotion posts each day. Share them to your personal page and as widely as you possibly can.

Party!

WEEK 52 ~ PERSEVERE

It's over, and it's just beginning.

Turn your writing attention to Book 2.

At least once a month—and once a week is preferable—schedule more blogs and posts about this first book, a minimum of one post a month, for the next four months. Talk about what you learned, the obstacles that you overcame, what you wish you had known when you started.

Connect your posts to events in the world at large. Tilt your head sideways when thinking of ways to promote your writing to the world.

Gradually transition to posts about your second book. Because you've started that, haven't you? Your goal now is to finish Book 2 in eight months, not 12.

You can go faster now. You know the process. You have a cover designer. You don't have to learn formatting. No wondering about how to do this or that. You've worked through this guide, and you're starting to abandon this guide as you make the novel writing process all your own.

When you start Book 3, try to finish it in 6 months, which means you can do 2 books in one year, and keep striving. With this third book, dip into advertising. After Book 3, consider short stories and novelettes in that world to publish as loss leaders (free introduction to the story or to the world you've built or to the character).

Everything that you've learned this year, you don't have to re-learn. However, when you get stuck, it's still all here, available to guide you—until you can climb the mountain without a guide.

I want to hear about your successes and the obstacles that you overcame. You can contact me at winkbooks@aol.com

Happy writing!

Raison d'Etre

How many miles have you traveled on the road to writing your novel? If you're not far on that road, if you keep backing up, if your engine stalls, if the myriad of roads confuse you, then *Discovering Your Novel* will help you drive through those problems.

No one else can write the novel of your head and heart. That's a road you have to find and follow. Yet this workbook, like a mountain guide, can lead your journey to publication.

Publication is the goal, isn't it? Not just to write but to share your writing through publication.

I ask because I recently met a NaNoWriMo[8] participant ecstatic about her eighth year of participation after "winning" for the previous seven years. Winning means that she achieved the word-count requirement. In seven years she'd written 350,000 words (minimum) yet still had nothing published.

350,000 words. Let that sink in. Most novels are around 75,000 words, with the epics around 120,000. That's at least four good-sized books, or three-plus epics. This writer may have submissions to agents and editors with traditional publishers or small presses. All I truly know is that she still wasn't published. 7 years & 350,000 words and not published.

Ouch.

I drove that road. I've written about my writing journey in earlier books. What you need to know is that I collected lots of rejection letters as I trundled along, sight-seeing like any tourist. Those rejection letters were like a t-shirt, a token of where I'd been. All of the later letters repeated something along the lines of "We like this but. . . .

- It's not romantic (or fantastical) enough.
- This doesn't fit our current catalog.
- We have too many similar books in our catalog.
- Mysteries set after World War I don't sell.
- Fantasies set in alternate medieval worlds don't sell.
- Regency mysteries don't sell.
- Please try again.

After a decade of those, I stopped submitting manuscripts. Oh, I kept writing. Occasionally, I tried again, but I had lost my earlier drive. I wrote the stories that I wanted to read rather than writing to market. The 18-to-24-month lag time for the road from acceptance to publication meant that the market was two years ahead of whatever was just released.

---

[8] NaNoWriMo = National Novel Writing Month, every year in November. The group that runs NaNoWriMo (pronounced Nano-Rhi-Moh) has a website with all sorts of templates for your perusal and playtime. Writers who sign up to participate have to write 50,000 words in one month, which is about 1666 daily.

Bad things happen to good people (and bad ones, just so you know). When I dragged myself from the mucky mire of grief, the Kindle revolution had changed the publishing world. Traditional publishing had shrunk, squeezing out midlist writers and grabbing copyrights and licensing rights rather than partnering with writers.

While traditional and small press publishers serve as gatekeepers who bestow a cachet of "worthiness", writers in that realm claw to retain their rights yet still must handle the majority of their marketing. Vanity publishers will take any writers who will pay them to publish, then take more money for distribution, and even more money for marketing packages.

Weigh indie publication against conglomerate & small press publishers and the pay-to-play vanity houses, and indie is a writer's new friend. Indies do handle everything themselves. Whatever they can't personally do, they can contract with copy editors, cover designers, printers, and distributors.[9] Amazon's Kindle Direct Publishing branch and similar entities are an indie writer's dream.

You pick the route you want to follow in your writing journey—traditional or indie or hybrid (traveling in both realms). Amanda Hocking is one highly successful indie writer who leaped into traditional publishing. Connie Brockway, highly successful in traditional publishing, announced that she will become self-published. Marie Force lives in both realms.

Whichever realm you decide to travel, best-selling status and megabucks are not guaranteed. Most indies who earned a great deal did so early in the ebook revolution. The market is now flooded with wannabees and has now matured. Fame and fortune are possible but not assured.

You may read one of my published novels and say, "I can do better." Go for it. Please. The only difference between you and me is that I found a road that would allow me to pursue my dream. What's preventing your dream? When you examine your life closely, when you look for one hour every night or four 15-minutes during the day, you will discover your dream is possible, too.

FIRST MAJOR QUESTION

What is your actual goal?

- I write to please myself. > Success guaranteed.
- I write to support myself. > No guarantees but possible once you develop a strong backlist.
- I write to get rich. > Definitely no guarantees.
- I write to become famous (or infamous). > Most definitely no guarantees. (Do you really want to be infamous?)

SECOND MAJOR QUESTION

How do you define yourself?

- I'm a writer.
- I'm a money-chasing schemer.
- I'm desperate for fame.

---

[9] Writers need to be wary when dealing with editors, designers, printers, and distributors. Just like the rest of the world, the writing field has unscrupulous money-grabbers eager to steal hard-earned dollars. Be careful out there.

We all yearn secretly for fortune and fame. Who doesn't?

Reality tells us that not everyone can be rich and famous. The ebook marketplace is flooded with great pro writers shifting their works into electronic publishing, out-of-print books finding new publication, reprints of enduring classics in the various genres, desperate wannabees and eager newbies, and money-chasing schemers.

What separates a pro writer from a newbie or a wannabe? Impetus. That's all. Be consistent and persistent, and soon you'll also be a pro writer.

If you want your books to endure and transfer into the newest incarnations decades from now, then your goal is great story-telling.

Writers of fiction *and* nonfiction need to be great story-tellers. Everything flows from that start.

This workbook is like a roadmap. Launch your writing journey at your current location on the road the publishing—incipient idea or character sketches or story plan or struggling manuscript or completed novel looking into publication.

Track progress with daily word counts and progress meters.

Learn the devices and definitions that pro writers have swirling in their heads.

Maintain the discipline and preparation that keeps pro writers at work, no matter the interruptions.

Each time we repeat the process from beginning to end, we internalize more and more of the skills.

Each time we write, we reach new clarity about stories, about life, and about ourselves.

Each time we finish and launch a book, we're traveling the road to pro. The next book is easier. As is the third. And the 10th. And the 20th.

Fifth book in, consider yourself a Pro. And keep writing.

Thank you for reading *Discovering Your Novel*. After years of teaching in the classroom, I really had a hard time turning off the teacher. The guidebooks that are part of the **Think like a Pro Writer** series are the result of that inability to shut up. Writing this book was pure pleasure. The words flew onto the page.

For any questions, comments, and speculations, please contact winkbooks@aol.com. You can find my books on my Amazon author page or my website ~~ www.writersinkbooks.com

I don't collect email addresses or use affiliate links. Nor will I bombard you with newsletters or the like. I've got writing to do, for all my books are my own. I don't use ghostwriters or work-for-hire writers or collaborators. Beta Readers and proofreaders, however, are always helpful. If you spot an error, please let me know. As soon as possible, I will correct it and re-upload, which will make available to you an updated novel file.

Indie writers thrive on reviews. With *any* book that you enjoy, please share with other readers looking for escape from the stresses of life.

Dream it. Believe it. Do it.

~~ M. A. Lee

NONFICTION BY M.A. LEE

Think like a Pro: New Advent for Writers

Think / Pro: A Planner for Writers An undated planner with daily word counts, progress meters, project planning, and goals analysis. Paperback only. How else will you record your goals and progress? Two different covers available.

Old Geeky Greeks: Write Stories with Ancient Techniques

Discovering Your Novel

Discovering Your Characters

Discovering Your Plot

Discovering Your Author Brand

Discovering Sentence Craft

Just Start Writing, **book 1 in the** *Inspiration 4 Writers* **series, written with Remi Black and Edie Roones**

*2 * 0 * 4 Lifestyle: Transform Your Whole Self* (coming soon)

*2 * 0 * 4 Lifestyle: A Planner for Living* Using Luke 10:27 for the whole self—heart, soul, mind & body—an undated planner to help you muse and move, feast and fast, and live and love. Paperback only. How else will you write in it? Seven covers available: Meadow (my favorite), Floral, Woodland (for hikers), Mountain River (my second favorite), Cityscape (with the Henley Street Bridge in Knoxville as the focus), Teatime (in the garden), and English Cottage (with spiced tea on the back cover).

HEARTS IN HAZARD BY M.A. LEE

Mysteries with a dash of romance, set during the Regency Era of England:

1 ~ *A Game of Secrets,* **published October 2015** ~ Smugglers, secrets and spies: Kate tries to hide in plain sight; Tony tries to catch a spy. First they fall in love; then they fall into trouble with smugglers. Will they survive?

2 ~ *A Game of Spies,* **published November 2015** ~ Salons and soirées, flirtation and dancing, gambling and spies: Josette and Giles fall in love over a deck of cards and try not to die.

Spymaster Giles Hargreaves was introduced in *A Game of Secrets.*

3 ~ *A Game of Hearts,* **published December 2015** ~ Two couples :: One titled widow, one wealthy businessman: two hearts shadowed by their past. One bright young flirt, one hard-edged young man: two hearts crossed by circumstance. Mix in a courtesan and two rakes, all out for mischief, and murder bloody and foul.

4 ~ *The Danger of Secrets,* **published February 2017** ~ Deep in the wintry countryside, a house warmed by relatives and friends: secrets of family, secrets of hearts, secrets of blood and pain. Match a daughter to an unknown father; match a spinster to an earl; match a serial killer to his next victim. (Gordon Musgrove was introduced in *A Game of Spies.*)

5 ~ *The Danger for Spies,* **published March 2017** ~ Impossible: rakes don't lose their hearts. Impossible: spies don't give up the game. Impossible: no one hides in plain sight. Impossible: codes are unbreakable. Impossible: a man can't hold onto revenge for years and years. Impossibilities are designed to be shattered. (Toby Kennitt was introduced in *A Game of Spies.*)

6 ~ *The Danger to Hearts,* **published April 2017** ~ A country manor in early Spring: older woman and younger man. Horses, cats, needlework, roses and afternoon teas ~ what could possibly go wrong in an idyll? Trouble in the past, trouble now, and murder. (The character Joss Carter was introduced in *A Game of Secrets.)*

7 ~ *The Key to Secrets,* **published January 2018** ~ Debutantes should snare fiancés, not murder them. Constable Hector Evans (from *The Danger to Hearts)* returns to solve three murders. Is his former love guilty of murder or a convenient scapegoat?

8 ~ *The Key for Spies,* **published January 2019** ~ Spies and traitors. Lies and treachery. Unexpected love where bullets fly. One traitor destroys loyalty. What will two traitors destroy?

9 ~ *The Key with Hearts* ~ A convenient marriage inconveniently causes murder.

10 ~ *The Hazard of Secrets* Two hearts with dangerous pasts. Can they keep their secrets, or will murder force them to reveal all?

11 ~ *The Hazard for Spies* ~ Disguised spies, disguised motives. When the masks are removed, will the truth be revealed? Or will murder result?

12 ~ *The Hazard for Hearts* ~Two wives haunt the castle. Will she become the third to die?

M.A. Lee also writes the **Into Death** Series, set after World War I

Digging into Death, published October 2016 ~ A governess seeking refuge, a handsome young man, an archaeological dig: romance is inevitable; murder is not. Suspicions escalate, artifacts are stolen, and then a second murder. Has the love of her life beguiled her straight into death? Available in paperback and e-book

Christmas with Death, published December 2017 ~ Christmas is for miracles, merriment, and murder. Set in 1919 at an English country manor for a party throughout Christmastide. Available in paperback and e-book.

Portrait with Death (in the sketching stage)

PEN NAMES OF M.A. LEE

❖ Remi Black, fantasy

Fae Mark'd Wizard

Weave a Wizardry Web

Dream a Deadly Dream

Sing a Graveyard Song

Wield a Fae-Sharpened Sword (in the sketching stage)

Kindle a Dragon's Fire (in the sketching stage)

Dance to Bone-Edged Music (in the sketching stage)

To Wield the Wind: **Fae Mark'd World**

❖ Edie Roones, medieval-style fantasy

The Seasons in Sansward Quarternary

Summer Sieges

Autumn Spells

Winter Sorcery

Spring Magicks (in the sketching stage)

All books from Writers' Ink are available at Amazon.

For any comments, questions, and speculations, contact winkbooks@aol.com. Use the subject line to direct your email to a specific book or series.

NOTES

www.ingramcontent.com/pod-product-compliance
Lightning Source LLC
Chambersburg PA
CBHW080556090426
42735CB00016B/3252